Mel Churcher

Mel Churcher was an actor and broadcaster for many years. Her work included leading roles with the Royal National Theatre, the New Shakespeare Company and extensive film, radio and television work.

She is now best known as an international acting, dialogue, voice and presentation coach and has run workshops and given lectures all over the world. She has worked in the voice department of the Royal Shakespeare Company, the Regent's Park Open Air Theatre (where she was Head of Voice and Text for twelve years), Shakespeare's Globe, the Young Vic, Manchester Royal Exchange, Birmingham Repertory Theatre and the Royal Court Theatre in London. She served on the Council of the British Voice Association.

Mel is also one of the top acting and dialogue coaches in movies. Her work includes *The Lady, The Door, The Last Station, Control, King Arthur, Danny the Dog / Unleashed, The Fifth Element, The Count of Monte Cristo* and *Lara Croft: Tomb Raider*, working with actors such as Gerard Butler, Daniel Craig, Stephen Dillane, Paul Giamatti, Angelina Jolie, Milla Jovovich, Keira Knightley, Jet Li, Mads Mikkelson, Clive Owen, Sam Riley, Stellan Skarsgåard, John Turturro, Jon Voight and Ray Winstone.

She runs screen acting workshops for professional actors around the world and regularly teaches in Cologne and Berlin and at the Actors Centre in London. Having directed and taught in most of the major London drama colleges, she still works with graduating students at LAMDA and Central School of Speech and Drama, where she advised on the setting up of the MA in Screen Acting. Mel is also a theatre director with her own company, Trojan's Trumpet.

Mel has an MA in Performing Arts (Mddx), an MA in Voice Studies (CSSD) and an Institute of Phonetics Association Diploma. She has written numerous articles on voice and her first book *Acting for Film: Truth 24 Times a Second* (Virgin Books, 2003) is now recommended reading for many major drama schools.

For more information, see www.melchurcher.com or Mel's entry on www.imdb.com.

A Screen Acting Workshop

MEL CHURCHER

Foreword by Jeremy Irons

NICK HERN BOOKS

London

www.nickhernbooks.co.uk

A Nick Hern Book

A Screen Acting Workshop
first published in Great Britain in 2011
by Nick Hern Books Limited, The Glasshouse,
49A Goldhawk Road, London W12 8QP

Reprinted 2013

Author photograph by Holger Borggrefe
Cover image by Shutterstock.com/Triff
Cover designed by www.energydesignstudio.com

Typeset by Nick Hern Books, London

Printed and bound in Great Britain by
Mimeo Ltd, Huntingdon, Cambridgeshire

A CIP catalogue record for this book is available
from the British Library

ISBN   978 1 84842 055 7

Woodland
CARBON
www.woodlandcarbon.co.uk
NICK HERN BOOKS
Printed on Carbon Captured paper

To Chris and Ben

Contents

Workshop 2: Inhabiting the Role 41

Workshop 3: The Physical Life 101

Foreword

Film acting has traditionally, in the UK at least, been rather looked down on as being something that the Americans do and which really doesn't need the technique of a theatre actor. In England, we're mainly theatre actors, and film actors have been historically regarded as overpaid and under-talented.

But in reality, film acting can give you a real insight into acting in the theatre, because you can't lie on film whereas you can get away with lying in theatre. In other words, the camera will see you if you are pretending. You have to *be*. Now, I believe you have to *be* in the theatre also. You have to have a technique to enlarge that state of 'being' so that an audience, whether it's two hundred or two thousand, can understand what you're saying and what you're thinking and what you're feeling. And you have to be able to transmit that. But in order to do that honestly, you have to be able to *be* in that moment – with no pretence. And if you come to film and think that you can 'pretend' in front of the camera (which you can get away with on stage, and which you see a lot of actors doing) – it doesn't work.

In life, we recognise the difference between someone pretending to be angry and someone *being* angry. We can tell whether they really find something funny or if they're pretending to find something funny. So, if we 'pretend' on stage, a perceptive audience can sometimes tell. Well – they can *always* tell on camera.

So I think film is a real testing ground for actors. You have to find ways to get, very quickly, into your role – to learn the techniques that you need when you're going to shoot, probably, in short little bites. You have to understand what the scene's about and what the arc of the scene is, as you would in theatre, but then you have to be able to get immediately into the right bit of that arc for the particular shot that's being done. These days, people tend to shoot longer takes, shoot wide and use multiple cameras, so things are easier than they were. But you've still got to have tricks to make sure that – very fast – you're ready. You don't want directors to have to do more than two or three takes. The old days of fourteen or fifteen takes are over.

The misunderstanding arises, I think, from people assuming film and television acting is no more than being 'real'. Hopefully you will seem to 'be', but you are being someone else in a different situation. You have to get yourself into that situation. Now some work doesn't require very much. Some work requires much more, requires you have to make a huge leap – into maybe a different century or to a personality that's completely different to you, the actor. I think great acting should be seamless. It shouldn't show. It's a god-given talent that some people have. I watch the great actors and try to learn from them.

Training is important. I think it's useful to get used to the situation on set – to get used to dealing with the pressure. People will say so often, 'Real people are so much more interesting than actors – let's have a *real* person playing that role.' And so you bring in a real person and you put the lights on them, turn on the camera, and they just collapse with nerves. What you have to do, as an actor, is to be used to all that tension and the time pressure, and learn not to worry about it.

Keep your own space. Know the jewel that you carry – what you have to offer, that no one else can do. Make sure you are in a completely calm space that is the right space for that moment in the scene. So that you don't *see* the camera, you don't *see* the lights, you don't *see* the technicians watching. That's clearly very important, and you will learn to do that with practice and training.

You have to allow the lens into you. You have to be open to it but not play for it. It's an attitude. When I say 'Keep your own space', it's about making the space to allow us to see what you're thinking, see what you're going through. Because storytelling is what we do in a film – sharing experience, sharing emotion. And people who put things *out* to you tend to make you, as an audience, pull back…

I've always thought that making a character is like making an advent calendar. In each scene, you open a window and you just show a bit of life inside that particular room from that angle, and then the next scene you open another window…

But *invite* us in. Don't feel you have to justify yourself or *show* yourself. You don't. Just intrigue us…

Jeremy Irons

Acknowledgements

I am deeply indebted to all my teachers and directors as an actor, and all my actors and colleagues as a teacher and director – with special mention to friends at the British Voice Association; to Cicely Berry, who is always my mentor; to Tim Reynolds, who gave me my first chance to direct; and to Luc Besson, who has provided me with some of my most exciting film projects.

A special thank-you to all the actors who bravely allowed me to use their private rehearsal work on the DVD, and to all the actors whose work it would have been wonderful to use if space had permitted.

Thank you to my publisher Nick Hern and to my editor Matt Applewhite for their tireless support and encouragement.

Thank you so much to Jeremy Irons for his clear and thoughtful Foreword.

Thanks to the Actors Centre (www.actorscentre.co.uk) and my colleagues there for all their help and assistance: Matthew Lloyd, Michael John, Diane Shorthouse, my long-suffering film editor Daniele Mercanti (who also devised the complex navigation system for the DVD), and DOP Ivan Dalmedo.

Thanks to Holger Borggrefe, Johanna Schenkel, DOP Andreas Kohler and sound mixer Gerd 'Ide' Lödige and all my colleagues at ifs international film school Cologne (www.filmschule.de).

Thanks to Interkunst e.V. in Berlin (www.interkunst.de) and my colleagues there: Til Dellers, Arkadiusz Zietek and DOP Matthias Kremer.

Thanks to Penelope Cherns at LAMDA and DOPs Alvin Leong and Nayla El-Solh.

Thanks to Amanda Brennan and Catherine Alexander at Central School of Speech and Drama and DOP Keir Burrows.

Thanks to Drew Stocker at Alleyn's School for providing the means for a workshop and to Ben C. Roose for organising it.

Thank you to sound mixer John Rodda and his kind colleagues for providing me with real studio sound effects.

Thank you to actors Daniela Holtz and John Keogh for permission to use extracts from their e-mails.

Thank you to Kevin MacLeod (www.incompetech.com) for the use of his music as credited on the DVD, and to Kirsty Mather for the use of her song.

…Last, but always first, love and thanks to Chris and Ben Roose.

Mel Churcher

The author and publisher also gratefully acknowledge permission to quote from the following, in the book and on the DVD:

China is Near by Marco Bellocchio, translated by Judith Green (copyright © 1969 Grossman Publishers, Inc.), published by Calder and Boyars (Publishers) Ltd; *Playing by Heart* by Willard Carroll, by kind permission of the author; *Savage in Limbo* by John Patrick Shanley, published by Dramatists Play Service, Inc.; *Junebug* by Angus MacLachlan, by kind permission of Epoch Films; *Girl, Interrupted* by James Mangold, *The Spider Men* by Ursula Rani Sarma, in *Shell Connections 2006: New Plays for Young People* and *Victory* by Harold Pinter in *Collected Screenplays: Vol. 2* (copyright © 2000 Harold Pinter), published by Faber and Faber Ltd; 'Three Women: A Poem for Three Voices' by Sylvia Plath in *Collected Poems*, published by Faber and Faber Ltd in the UK (copyright © 1989 The Estate of Sylvia Plath), and in *Winter Trees*, published by HarperCollins Publishers in the US (copyright © 1968 Ted Hughes); 'Burnt Norton' from *Four Quartets* by T.S. Eliot, published by Faber and Faber Ltd in the UK, and by Houghton Mifflin Harcourt Publishing Company in the US (copyright © 1936 by Harcourt, Inc., renewed 1964 by T.S. Eliot); *The Freedom of the City* by Brian Friel, by kind permission of the author and The Gallery Press; *To the Actor* by Michael Chekhov, published by Harper and Row; clips from Ministry of Information films, by kind permission of the Imperial War Museum; *The Naked Civil Servant* by Philip Mackie; *The Silence* from *A Film Trilogy* by Ingmar Bergman, translated by Paul Britten Austin (copyright © 1963 Ingmar Bergman, this translation © 1978 Marion Boyars Publishers Ltd), and *Face to Face* by Ingmar Bergman, translated by Alan Blair (copyright © 1976 Ingmar Berman, this translation © 1976 Alan Blair), both published by Marion

Boyars Publishers Ltd; *Beautiful People* by Scott Rosenberg; *Building a Character* and *Creating a Role* by Constantin Stanislavsky, translated by Elizabeth Reynold Hapgood, *The Cut* by Mike Cullen and *The Memory of Water* by Shelagh Stephenson, published by Methuen Drama, an imprint of A&C Black Publishers Ltd; *Eternal Sunshine of the Spotless Mind* by Charlie Kaufman (copyright © 2004 Universal Studios Licensing LLLP), *Honour* by Joanna Murray-Smith, *Low Level Panic* by Clare McIntyre, and *The Treatment* by Martin Crimp, all published by Nick Hern Books Ltd; *On Acting* by Sanford Meisner (copyright © 1987 Sanford Meisner and Dennis Longwell), published by Random House Books; cartoons from *Will Write and Direct for Food* by Sir Alan Parker (copyright © 2005 Alan Parker), published by Southbank Publishing, by kind permission of the artist; *Departure Lounge* by Lorna Holder, by kind permission of Lorna Holder of Tuareg Productions; and *The Constant Gardener* by Jeffrey Caine (copyright © 2005 Focus Features), by kind permission of Universal Studios Licensing LLLP.

Every effort has been made to contact copyright holders. The publisher will be glad to make good in any future editions any errors or omissions brought to their attention.

Using this Book and DVD

What follows in this book is based on my five-day Acting for Screen workshops, and the accompanying DVD shows real moments that happened during some of these workshops. The filming was not set up for the purposes of the DVD – hence the variable technical quality of the clips. Because the actors were genuinely involved in their work, the examples have an immediacy that would not have been possible to replicate in a controlled environment.

The DVD is designed to enhance and elucidate the text by providing examples and visual references. You may view it as you wish but, initially, I would suggest that you watch each workshop all the way through on the DVD *after* reading that chapter in the book. Alternatively, you can use the two side by side, watching exercises and examples on the DVD as they are described in the book.

In the book, the DVD symbol alerts you to the relevant part of the DVD so that you can return to it whenever you wish. Separate sections are indicated by Workshop Number then Scene Number, so that ⊙ **3.8**, for example, refers to Workshop 3 ('The Physical Life'), Scene 8 ('Toybox: Circling') on the DVD. From time to time, I shall also add clips to my website that might be of interest: www.melchurcher.com

You'll hear a few instances of strong language on the DVD as the actors use examples from modern scripts, so please be aware that you might not consider it appropriate for younger viewers. It's infrequent, though, and shouldn't cause any worries for anyone familiar and comfortable with the average television drama after 9 p.m.

*'Qui vit sans folie
n'est pas si sage qu'il croit.'*

'He who lives without folly
is not as wise as he thinks.'

Rochefoucault (1613–80)

Workshop 1

Introduction

I was an actor once, so I know what it's like to go in front of the camera. I know about the actor's nightmares the night before filming, the butterflies in the stomach, the panic that rises when you forget your lines, the dry mouth, the racing heart, and the performance that's over before it began.

A long time ago, I started teaching and directing and trying to calm other people who were going through what I used to experience. I began to see how the responsibility of trying to be 'good actors' was getting in their way. How seeking a feedback that they were really 'feeling' was leading to the opposite effect. How when they said it felt 'too easy', it had suddenly become real and powerful.

I first worked as an acting coach on a film around twenty years ago and since then I've been standing around on a set for months at a time, watching the monitor for twelve hours a day on more than forty major films and television productions. I have been lucky enough to see many different directors at work and to watch how the actors' performances grew and changed with the input of those around them. I have also taught thousands of actors and would-be actors in

3

workshops and studios both in groups and in one-to-one sessions. Out of this work came my first book, *Acting for Film: Truth 24 Times a Second*, which is a thorough overview of all aspects of film acting. Now, I want to share my practical workshops, designed to prepare you further for your work on camera – work that is not only magic and instant but also long and tedious.

Marlon Brando said, 'Acting is the least mysterious of all crafts. Whenever we want something from somebody or when we want to hide something or pretend, we're acting. Most people do it all day long.'

Drama schools are a wonderful way to train, but they also fill you with so much information that it is sometimes hard to let it go in the moment of performance. You have to trust that, once you have done all the homework, you simply need to believe in the situation and 'be there'. Just do what you need to get what you want – like life. And let the preparation take care of itself. You need to be able to go back to having total belief in your imagination as you did when you were five and knew that the ghosts were after you at the bottom of the garden, or the spaceship would arrive at any moment to whisk you away, or that the area under the hedge was the hut you had built on your tropical island. ✇ **Introduction**

Most of us run around through life worrying about the future or dwelling on the past. Whatever your role is doing, you, the actor, have to be in the here and now in order to inhabit that role. It is a precious accomplishment to stop time. The actor and director Maria Aitken says of comedy, 'There is only one moment and that moment is now'; D. H. Lawrence talked constantly of 'the living moment'; Eckhart Tolle wrote a bestselling book called *The Power of Now*, and to quote T.S. Eliot's poem 'Burnt Norton':

❝ What might have been and what has been
   Point to one end, which is always present.

An actor has to find that power – to stop time, to be present in the present. That is the joy of our work. That is why we train.

If training hardens into one 'technique' or 'method', it ceases to be fluid and personal. You have to find what works for you and create your own perfect mix. Over time, by being eclectic and going down many different routes, I've discovered what I find the most helpful advice for actors working on screen:

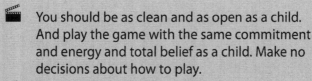

   You should be as clean and as open as a child. And play the game with the same commitment and energy and total belief as a child. Make no decisions about how to play.

   You need to find ways to engage your whole body in that game, to store specific muscle memory, pictures and sense awareness. It is not enough simply to think about the part.

   You have to separate the preparation from the doing. You add to your subconscious during preparation, and you are solely in the present, engaging with your role's conscious thoughts, during playing.

   You have, at the deepest level, to be working from yourself. Which brings us back to my first point. Children are not confused. They play their roles as if they themselves *are* the roles. Then they stop and go to tea.

What would I most like you to experience in the moment of doing your work in front of the camera? A freedom, an ease, a simplicity, a spontaneity and a release from knowing and deciding. To be as free in 'the moment of now' as you should be in life. It is as if you stand by a closed door, knowing where you belong in the world, knowing who might be waiting inside, responding to a need that makes you open the door and go in. But with no knowledge of what will happen next.

The Natural versus the Unnatural

Playing, imagining, empathising is natural. The child plays through the imagination and belief in the situation that the game has conjured up. We care for others because our imaginations say, 'What if I were in this situation...?'

Reading squiggles on a page, learning the words they represent and then having to speak them exactly as they are written is not like life. Being asked to move to a particular spot, gesticulate in a certain way and then speak those lines of love in front of a camera and several hundred technicians is not natural.

In life, we never speak or move without an impulse, a need. To take prescribed words and moves and then to have a need so strong and so precise that it can only result in those words and moves is an unnatural act.

No one can teach you the natural but the unnatural can be learnt. You can wake up the child in you to release the natural and acquire the unnatural craft of the expert you must become. You need to mix the folly and bravery of the child with the wisdom of the sage. And it will be a joyful lifelong endeavour!

You are Unique

Nobody does 'you' like you. You are unique. You are your best asset. When you go to an audition, you are not in competition with other actors. Only you can offer your particular viewpoint of the world, your embodiment of the role. The other actors are offering their unique visions. Which version the director chooses to buy is a different matter. You may not get the part but it is as if the director chooses Aphrodite over Athene or Dionysus over Apollo, the Nile over the Tigris or the Thames over the Loire, Brando over Bogarde or Garbo over Monroe. Although only one person can be chosen for the role, no one else will play it like you. So no one is competing with the way you will play it.

What you must do is release the brakes you put on yourself. You need to trust your power of belief and thought. You need to believe that you and the role are one. Then your interpretation of the part will come fully alive and the director can make an informed decision. Directors are not psychic and can't see the talent inside you unless it is revealed. And when you get the part, you want the role to be as alive and extraordinary and unique as you are yourself.
🎧 1.0, 1.1

See how alive people's eyes and faces are in life! As Georgia talks about her quarry dive, the pictures in her head are so strong that she uses gestures all the time to recreate them for her audience and in reaction to what she sees and how she feels about it. Ana's eyes move upwards as she sees the pictures in her head again. Notice how, as she empathises with the dog's plight, she actually 'becomes' the dog. Will feels his fear again as he sees the bungee jump he has to do. He feels the rope around his ankles and sees the drop beneath him. Marion relives her ordeal moment by moment. Watch her 'see' the big ship and then her son and dog in her canoe. Daniela relives the absurdity of her story even before she tells it and the vivid pictures it evokes make her laugh helplessly – so we laugh too.

What About the Character?

Scripts with an Arc

'*...so you see Max, I'm really you and you're really me...*'

'I'm a dude playing a dude disguised as another dude – you're a dude who don't know what dude he is.' So says Robert Downey Jnr. as Kirk Lazarus in the film *Tropic Thunder* (2008).

I'm going to be controversial here. I hate the word 'character' – as in, 'finding my character' or 'it's a character part'. I

8

do end up saying it occasionally in the course of a workshop because it's sometimes hard to find an alternative – but I prefer the word 'role'.

So often, when actors think of their 'characters', it is as if they hold up a cardboard cut-out in front of themselves. 'My character...' they say, 'My character would/wouldn't do this or that... he or she is not like that... he is a bastard, she is sweet...' They talk about the 'character' as an idea in the third person and often judgementally – 'She is in love with a romantic ideal', 'He is a bit of a nerd.' Is the role really so self-aware that they could say that of themselves? Or are you simply standing outside looking in at the 'character', instead of being in their shoes? What if it was *you* – you 'as if' you've led the life they've led and are in this situation now?

I've lost count of the times that someone has come to me through a casting director or an agent because, although they are so right for the role, they never get cast. This person sits in my front room, beautiful, sexy and a bit edgy and I think, 'Why are they here when they are already eminently castable?' Then they pick up the script and the interesting human being in front of me vanishes. Suddenly, there's a very ordinary, very needy, two-dimensional creature reading a script too fast, a little high-pitched, leaning forward towards me.

'Why have you changed your posture/voice/attitude?' I ask.

'Because the character would be younger/needier/tired/sad and so on...'

But you, yourself, are so much more interesting than that, would be my comment.

So I film them talking about themselves and their recent encounters and they are always exciting to watch. Their eyes sparkle. They light up when they talk about something they are passionate about, or someone they love. And you can see them 'seeing' them. There is humour in their eyes, warmth, a little cynicism. They laugh when they tell you the sad things. Their voices are alive and connected.

Then I ask them to go into a monologue they know. Instantly, as I watch the monitor, the face drops, the eyes go dead, the humour drains away and the voice is disconnected.

We play back the recording. They are always amazed. 'Which is more interesting?' I ask. But we both know the answer. 💿 1.3

You can see the life draining out of people when they begin the unnatural task of speaking text and how it comes back vividly when they allow *themselves* back into the work. 💿 1.4

Thinking of the 'character' can block you.

Staying Alive

The trouble is, as actors, we want to be good. We are responsible people and we try really hard. We want to know we are being honest. We concentrate on whether we 'feel' real rather than on what we want or what we are trying to do.

But in life, when we have emotional feelings, we generally ignore them in order to pursue what we want. We don't sit around trying to 'feel'. The feeling happens anyway but it is a consequence of, or a side issue to, the business of pursuing our actions. We shouldn't be striving for some reassurance that we are connecting up with our feelings because that sends the energy back into ourselves instead of out into the world.

When we interact with others and the world around us, our energy goes *outwards* to deal with the situation. When we meet an obstacle, we try to get what we want in a different way. For example, if you asked your lover, 'Do you love me still?' your energy would not be directed at how you feel. That would happen of its own accord. What you would be doing would be watching and listening for every lie, every sign of unfaithfulness or for the comforting reassurance of love. If your lover evaded the question, that would be an obstacle that prevented you getting your need, so you would try to get this reassurance by taking a different action. You might try hugging them, hitting out, running away hoping they will chase you, or simply asking the question again. But you would take action in the immediacy of that specific moment. You wouldn't stop to check you were 'feeling something'. Yet that is what many actors do all the time, even if they aren't fully aware of it.

When actors are really connected to the moment, they say, 'It feels too easy, I don't feel anything is happening.' But when they see the work back, they find to their amazement that so much more is actually happening than when they were 'trying hard'. When I run workshops for directors I always warn them that when they get a great spontaneous take, the actor will come to them afterwards and ask them to go again because they 'didn't feel anything'!

 Get a friend to film you talking about a real experience about which you have clear memories and pictures of what happened. Talk to your friend holding the camera, don't look straight into the lens. Your friend can interject comments and questions as they wish.

 Watch your eyes light up with the memories and when you mention people you love, the way you smile before the words come out. Look how your eyes flick upwards to see the pictures in your head, how geographical you are, how physical you are, your tendency to laugh at the worst part of the story. See how alive you are. See how well you listen!

🎬 Go back in front of the camera and start recounting your real experience again. Now go seamlessly into delivering a monologue you know. Watch for your eyes going dead, how the humour at the side of your eyes can disappear. Is your voice as resonant or has it become thinner in tone, lower in volume? Are you now fixed in a gaze at your friend or are your eyes still seeing those pictures in your head and the world around you? Have you started to crane forward, is your face moving more, are your eyes screwing up?

🎬 Keep going back and forth between the learnt lines and the real story until you can see the life come back. Maybe it was a funny story and the monologue was sad – try it with the same energy. Is that possible? Could it be more interesting? In the role, could you still have a sense of irony, an awareness of the absurdity of it all? Do you prefer to watch it that way? If your real story was sad, did the way you told it surprise you? Would you have told it like that if you had seen it written down for the first time on the page?

🎬 Be brave; don't go into the monologue with fixed ideas. Try to keep *your* life and view of the world. Have the same energy on the learnt lines as when you were recounting real events.

Keep seeing how alive people are as themselves. 💿 **1.1, 1.2**

Nature and Nurture: You 'As If...'

You are your only instrument. When you are running it is *your* legs, *your* heart pumping, *your* blood pressure going up. When you touch the props, it is with *your* fingers. And when you think, it is *your* memories, imagination and feelings that are involved.

Stanislavsky talked about the power of the 'magic if' acting as a lever to lift us out of the world of actuality into the realm of imagination. So you could change just one element away from your actual experience, such as: '*If* it were three in the morning.' Or you could change many: '*If* it were 1609, *if* you had just killed your rival, *if* you had a humped back...'

You need to 'endow' yourself with the qualities you need within the imagined life of the role. For example, you could endow yourself with the quality of beauty or confidence or wealth. You could endow yourself with a limp or a lost love or a house in the country. You could endow the glass of water in your hand with the qualities of wine. Or you could say, '*If* I were now drinking wine...' The role is you 'as if'.

Sometimes confusion arises around the concept of 'playing yourself'. When I say that the role is you, that doesn't mean that it is necessarily your habitual physical self. The 'magic if' holds within it all the changes that would arise within you from being in a different time, having led a different life in a different world. The 'magic if' could affect very little or it could affect every aspect of your physical self and completely change the way you speak, hold your body or even your body itself. For example, if you were playing a role of the same age, living where you live and set in the present time, your main 'if' might be, '*If* I were in love with my best friend's wife...' But if your role were a vampire, your 'magic ifs' would be a long list: '*If* I needed the taste of blood like a drug...', '*If* I knew daylight would kill me...', '*If* I lived alone in the cold earth all day...', and so on. And your different needs will affect the way you interact with your new world.

But that doesn't mean that the core of you, your essence, disappears. And it doesn't mean that you need to change qualities that you share with the role. If, as is often the case in television, you are playing someone who lives in the same place and time as you, and is roughly the same age with a similar background – then you need only to believe in the given circumstances of the scene. If you are lucky enough to be given a role that is very different to yourself, then you need to find those differences. But you need to find them by believing that it is you standing in the shoes of the role. Not standing outside of the character, showing us an image of them as if you are conjuring up some hologram of the part. The inner life that powers your creation must be you yourself and your imagination.

Of course I'm not the first acting teacher to have said this. Let Stanislavsky explain:

> **❝** Each person evolves an external characterisation out of himself, from others, takes it from real or imaginary life, according to his intuition, his observation of himself and others. He draws it from his own experience of life or that of his friends, from pictures, engravings, drawings, books, stories, novels, or from some simple incident – it makes no difference. The only proviso is that while he is making this external research he must not lose his inner self.
>
> Constantin Stanislavsky
> *Building a Character*

Or, Sanford Meisner:

❝ The first thing you have to do when you read a text is to find yourself – *really* find yourself. First you find yourself, then you find a way of doing the part which strikes you as being in character. Then, based on that reality, you have the nucleus of the role.

Sanford Meisner
On Acting

Choose a few actors that you enjoy watching in a number of different roles. It might be an actor as chameleon-like as Philip Seymour Hoffman or Alec Guinness. It might be someone who plays across many different genres like Johnny Depp, Cate Blanchett, Emily Blunt or Kate Winslet. Now, ask yourself this: 'Do I believe them in the many different roles they play?' If you answer 'yes', then ask this: 'Do I ever go to the movie and feel cheated because they weren't really there?'

Whether a good actor plays many different kinds of roles or generally the same kind is a different issue. That may be due to market forces or a disinclination to vary roles, but in either case the 'core' of the actor is always there.

When watching clips of herself at an awards ceremony, Judi Dench said that she hated watching herself because she felt that she always looked the same. That is because she could see the truth of herself in every clip. But equally, each role showed a different facet of herself: a different physicality and a different view on the world. Whether she is playing an embittered lonely schoolteacher in *Notes on a Scandal* (2006), Queen Victoria in *Mrs Brown* (1997) or a modern working woman in the television sitcom *As Time Goes By* (1992), she is totally believable as the role but still, essentially, Judi Dench. She doesn't short-change us.

Think about putting on different clothes. They can change the way we look, the way we move, even the way we speak. They can change the way we interact with others. They even make us feel different. But it is always us inside, wearing them.

Look at the way we interact with different people in our lives. How we move between the role of parent, child, teacher and employee. How differently we act, hold our bodies and deal with our status in each situation. And yet, which one is really us? All of them, surely.

A child doesn't say, 'This character's Superman – he can fly.' The child says, '*I'm* Superman – *I* can fly!'

When you first read a script, you are allowed to analyse it and to think about your role objectively:

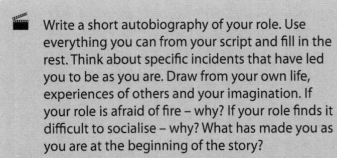

Write a short autobiography of your role. Use everything you can from your script and fill in the rest. Think about specific incidents that have led you to be as you are. Draw from your own life, experiences of others and your imagination. If your role is afraid of fire – why? If your role finds it difficult to socialise – why? What has made you as you are at the beginning of the story?

Make a list of all the similarities between you and your role and all the things that are different. You only have to find the differences.

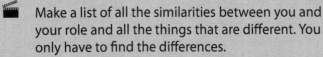

Work on the differences. If you are playing a doctor, you need to know the life you lead. You need to be able to use the instruments, relate to the nurses, and deal with the patients. You do it every day. Suppose it is set in 1860 – you need to know about that world. What art do you like? What music do you hear? What do you do for entertainment? How do you relate to people of a different sex, class or nationality? What are your

political views? Do you have any? How does a
corset change your movement? And so on.

 Find pictures, music or objects to inspire you. If
you are living in a different period, then you need
to research it thoroughly: museums and art
galleries are good places to start. If you are
somewhere you've never been, then go to a travel
agent and pick up a brochure on the place to
make what you see in your imagination more
specific. Or at least search for it online. Or 'endow'
somewhere you do know with those qualities. If
the place doesn't exist – you must make it exist.
Actors who talk about places, people or events in
the lives of their roles without having the least
idea of what or who they are always amaze me. Be
warned – the camera will see no life or light in
your eyes if you do that!

Now you need to come out of your head to explore your
physical reality. To work through your body and instincts.
To know the way of life that has shaped you.

 After your initial digging into the script, when
thinking through your part, always say 'I' rather
than 'she' or 'he'. Why complicate your life by
separating yourself from your role? By saying 'he'
or 'she' you are standing outside the role, looking
in. So, 'I hate my boss', 'It terrifies me to leave the
house', 'I want him to love me', and so on... **1.4**

 You need to explore the day-to-day life you lead.
How does it affect you physically? How does it
affect the way you speak? The way you move?

Which senses are important to your life? A gardener, a watchmaker, a hunter, a pianist, a skater will have developed different senses.

 Find a physical activity that you feel your role would do. Something that allows you to enter the life you will inhabit, such as embroidering, whittling a stick, arranging flowers or collecting stamps. This can also be a useful way of getting back into the role when you have had large gaps in filming.

 Remember that not all roles are naturalistic. (Think of some of Johnny Depp's!) For these you have to find a heightened physicality – through physical metaphors, dancing, singing or anything else you can think of. Find that child within you – children have no problems with superheroes or fantastical creatures!

Some actors simply feel that they 'channel' the 'character' through themselves, or act as mediums for the role to take over. That is another way to look at it. It is still using yourself and not imposing a character from the outside. It is still allowing yourself to inhabit or embody this new role and to give yourself permission to enter fully into new, brave territory.

Stepping into the Role

Actors can block themselves by standing outside their roles or having preconceived ideas – by relinquishing these and by taking on the role's viewpoint, they release their acting.
1.4

If you still feel separated from, or judgemental about, your role when you have done your preparation, try this:

- Shut your eyes and see him or her in a magic circle in front of you. View them as if you were standing behind them. Really observe them.

- Now see them as if you were playing the role. Study the back of your imagined self in great detail. See how you are dressed, stand and move. Hear yourself speak.

- Now take a step forward and literally step into the role. Open your eyes. Now you and the role have become indivisible. You see the world from their point of view – as 'I'. The needs of the role are your needs. The actions you will take are your actions.

- Speak your thoughts aloud. Speak your dialogue. Move out of your circle and into your imaginary world.

This is an excellent physical metaphor to stop you viewing your character as a third person.

All of this work applies to acting in every medium, but for camera work it is crucial. Anything false or untrue will show glaringly on the screen. And the fine work you learn to do in front of the camera will inform your work on stage. Sometimes we get away with things on stage that we can't in front of the camera. When you return to theatre, you will feel a new power and reality there too.

For further reading, I recommend the chapter in Stanislavsky's *Creating a Role* called 'The Period of Physical Embodiment', and I quote him once again:

> **❝** An actor can alter the circumstances of the life portrayed... he can develop habits in his role which are not native to him, and methods of physical

portrayal as well, and he can change his mannerisms, his exterior. All this will make the actor seem different in every role to the audience. But he will always remain himself too.

Constantin Stanislavsky
Creating a Role

Differences Between Stage and Screen

This is a good moment to analyse the differences between stage and screen, since most actors will have gone to drama school or university where the emphasis is primarily on stage acting or will have been drawn to performing by appearing in school plays or entertaining friends and family. It is true that the basic building blocks of acting are the same in both media. But some of the demands made by screen will take even experienced theatre actors by surprise and there is little preparation for them at present in the way most actors are trained. There are many important differences between stage and screen, but let's start with the big three:

1. There is no audience
2. You work out of order
3. You rehearse alone

1. There is No Audience

This really is the biggest one. It permeates the work at the subtlest level imaginable. Because, for most of us, performing has always been tied up with performing *to* somebody. So we have to take ourselves back to 'child's play', the private imaginative world that you used to inhabit. It is fascinating that in many languages the word for performing in a drama is the same word as that used for having fun: to play, *jouer*, *spielen*, *giocare*, *leka*, *spille*, and so on.

You have to make your imagination so strong that you can inhabit a real world where only you and the other characters exist. *There is no audience watching you.* It is like life, except that you are being closely observed by a camera. Indeed, you may be invaded by the camera.

Let's be clear about this. That camera is not an audience. You don't want to hide from the camera; you have to allow it to observe you. But you mustn't play to it.

The director is not your audience either. He or she is usually tucked away behind a monitor, watching, and is not concerned with the physical actuality of you on the set, but with your two-dimensional image inhabiting the screen world.

The crew is certainly not an audience and you need to resist any desire to play to them. They are there, involved in their own particular expertise. They don't really know or even care about how you do your work – the property master is looking at the props to check they are right, the costume designer is evaluating the clothes and the sound mixer is listening for passing aeroplanes.

Most of the crew can't even hear you (and shouldn't be able to if you are talking to another actor who's two feet away). Only the few people with headphones will hear you: the producer (who's thinking of the budget), the script supervisor (who's listening to check you're keeping to the script), the sound department (who are still searching for the mysterious hum), and the director – who is the only one wondering whether he or she believes you or not.

It is hard for us not to want to find an audience. I was working with a really experienced stage actor on a new television series, and he confessed that he was finding filming really hard because he felt that he needed to show the crew that he was a good actor. This was very honest of him and is likely to apply to most of us when we are insecure in a new situation.

But we need to fight that desire to 'show' anyone anything. At the moment of acting, we must allow our game-playing self to truly believe that there is no world outside our imaginative reality.

You need only to think, and to think at every moment (just as we do in life). If you try to *show* us what you are thinking, however subtly – you've added an audience. If you try to show the subtext (when you don't want the other character to see it) – you've added an audience. If you speak 'past' the other person in the scene to reach somewhere else – you've added an audience. And we won't believe you. And, actually, I don't think any of the above work for you on stage either. It is just that you might get away with cheating more easily. And, as I've suggested, what you learn about truth by working on camera can be taken back to your stage work. I was watching some clips of Judi Dench showing her work both on stage and screen, and she is equally honest in both.

So to avoid a hidden audience:

> 🎬 Think hard and trust that is enough. Don't show us what you are thinking. 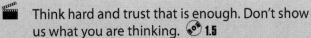 **1.5**
>
> 🎬 Pursue what you want. Make it crucial to get it. Don't show us how it affects you – just get on with getting it.
>
> 🎬 Don't colour your voice with emotion. That is you viewing the scene from the outside. Just speak as you would to get what you want or hide what you feel. If you watch people talking on the news or a documentary about the most terrible things, you will hear how factual they are. They don't need to show you what they feel; they just set about telling you the facts. Naturally, feelings may well up, but they deal with them to get on with the task.

Of course, you hope that an audience will see your work one day. But that is at a future point after the director and editor have recreated the work out of all the raw footage that has been shot. When the viewers see flickering images on a screen or watch the lit box in the corner of the room, you will not actually be there. And this audience has nothing to do with you and your work on set.

Theatre Dynamics

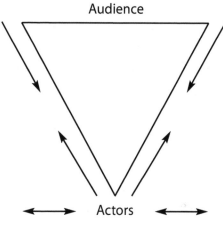

Screen Dynamics

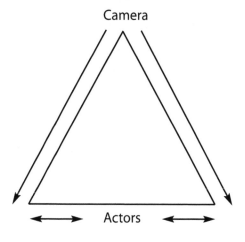

Above is a visual representation of the difference in the dynamics between actors and audience and actors and camera. In the first diagram (for theatre) the actors are at the apex of the triangle and they radiate energy between themselves and outwards towards the audience on the wide end of the triangle – shown by the directional arrows both between the actors and between the actors and audience. The arrows from the audience towards the actors represent their gaze. The arrows in this diagram go in both directions.

In the second diagram (for screen) the actors operate at the wide end of the triangle and the camera is at the apex. The directional arrows go between the actors and from the camera to the actors. The actors receive the camera's inanimate gaze. They allow it to observe them. But there are no arrows in the direction of actors to camera.

Will you miss the audience? The release from an audience can be a thrilling and liberating one – that return to the fantasy world you knew as a child. I hope you will often return to theatre to experience the immediate contact and two-way traffic that you have on stage, but there are parts of your work even there where an audience shouldn't exist.

The great theatre and film actor Michael Redgrave was asked whether he missed an audience when working on screen. He answered, 'Why should I? I do not miss an audience at rehearsals when the character is being created, and some of the most exciting moments of creative acting take place at rehearsals.' 👁 **1.5**

Jack 'shows' us what he is thinking and then simply thinks. If you look carefully you can see the subtle shifts but, like life, they *are* subtle. There is no audience to share them with.

2. You Work Out of Order

One of the reasons that it's great to act in theatre is that you have the luxury of working through the story in linear fashion. Each night you start at the beginning and finish at the end – and then go to the pub. Each night the journey is subtly different but the framework is the same.

In film and television, very rarely do you film scenes in order. This is for logistical reasons – you shoot all the scenes that are set in the same location together, do the night scenes in blocks or work around the availability of the leading actors.

So you are constantly moving around in time and space – arriving at the North Pole before you've left home, burying a lover before you've met them, killing your enemy before you've signed up for the Secret Service. Sometimes you go back to scenes that you have shot months before – or even longer. For example, Andy Serkis has said that his last day on set as Gollum in *The Lord of the Rings* trilogy (2001–3) was actually completing a scene which had started shooting on his first day on the set, four years before!

Here are some simple suggestions to prepare for this filmic jigsaw puzzle:

 First, read the whole script thoroughly – not just your scenes. You'd be surprised how many actors check only their own lines! Ridiculous – but we are all tempted to do it. (This tendency is particularly prevalent amongst actors who have only a small scene or are in a long-running television series.)

 Jot down a short synopsis of the plot.

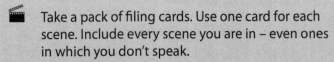

- Take a pack of filing cards. Use one card for each scene. Include every scene you are in – even ones in which you don't speak.

- Write the scene number on the top right-hand side. (The scene number is less likely to change than the page number.)

- Now write where you have come from at the top of the card and where you are going to at the bottom of the card.

- Add the time of day and where you are.

- Write down what you want or need in the scene – what drives you.

- Put in all the other characters in the scene with you and anything particular that you feel or know about them at that time, such as 'I've just found out she's pregnant', 'I'm beginning to suspect he's having an affair', etc.

- Put in any particular circumstances like the fact that it is stifling hot, that you've still got a sore left foot, that you're hungry, etc.

- Don't bother with the text – that's in the script. Now tether all the cards together with a ribbon or a piece of string. Now you have a flick book of your journey through the film. If scenes get added, you simply add a card. If one gets cut, you remove the card.

Don't neglect the instruction to write down where you arrive from. You are not coming onto set to play a scene. You are inhabiting a real life, which, from time to time, we film. The marvellous television actor Peter Barkworth (who also wrote two excellent books on acting) would come into a scene finishing some other business, like putting a handkerchief away – having blown his nose. You felt he really was coming from somewhere specific. The film actor Herbert Lom says that his first director told him his most valuable advice: to know where you're coming from and where you're going to.

You may wonder why you don't write all this information directly into your script. Well, television tends to stick to a few drafts but movies go through many, many versions. When a screenplay is ready for shooting, it is known as a 'locked script'. Every revision that is made after that arrives on a different coloured paper. The script that happens to be on my table at the moment is *Defiance* (2008). The 'locked script' was in May 2007. It then went through many revisions in different colours: blue, pink, yellow, green, goldenrod, salmon, cherry, buff, tan and then through the colours again all the way to cherry between June and October 2007. That makes seventeen different scripts and part-scripts before the film was completed. And that is, by no means, exceptional. So, by the time you've written your notes on the first three scripts, you will give up transferring them. Also a script is bulky to carry around and you will probably prefer to use the smaller A5 'sides' which contain the latest dialogue changes and are issued on each day of the shoot.

Preparing these cards will also ensure that you do detailed homework on the scenes. You will feel secure and prepared and, if the order of the scenes changes at the last moment, you have only to flick through your cards to know where you are in the plot. When you arrive at the set at six in the morning and find out that it blew down in the night and they are not shooting Scene Thirty, but Scene Sixty-two, you will not panic. You will calmly take out your cards, see where you are in the plot and brush up your lines in make-up.

If your role has a specific goal to reach or is experiencing continuing or progressive changes, you may want to go further than the cards and produce a graph. For example, when I worked with Jet Li on the film *Unleashed/Danny the Dog* (2005), Jet had to change from acting as a dog into becoming a man – both physically and mentally. We had a graph on the wall of his trailer that plotted his path from dog to man, and where he fell back from his journey, scene by scene. This meant that, at any moment during filming, he knew exactly where he was both physically and emotionally.

You need only to think of the twists and turns in *Eternal Sunshine of the Spotless Mind* (2004) or how Martin Sheen's role evolves in *Apocalypse Now* (1979) to see how important it would be to know where you were on those journeys. But it can be equally useful for the five scenes between breaking your leg and being fully healed! After all, out of order means out of continuity – so anything that helps solve that problem must be useful. What the actor needs to know (but the role must not) is the route this journey will take and the destination it will reach. You in the role must stay naïve – only knowing where you've come from, where you want to go and the moment that is 'now'.

3. You Rehearse Alone

One of the most difficult things about screen acting is the lack of rehearsal. You will arrive on the set, sometimes meet your playing partner for the first time, and then have to produce the perfect performance after one short run-through of the scene.

This is one of the conundrums of filming. How do you arrive at the set fully prepared and ready to give the performance of your life, yet without having made any decisions about how to play it, so you remain free and open to react in the moment and to feed off the other actors – actors whom you may not even have met before you begin shooting?

If there are any rehearsals for film they are not, to echo *Star Trek*, as you or I know them. Even in television you are unlikely to encounter more than a few days of rehearsal for high-end dramas, whilst on soaps and series, you will get none. Some film directors who come from a theatre background do have a pre-production period. But, unless there is a tiny cast, not all the actors will be there. A few smaller-budget productions may manage some real rehearsal time (I was lucky enough to be involved in some proper rehearsals for the 2007 film *Control*). But directors like Mike Leigh, who have a long rehearsal time before shooting, are rare.

Most of the time, if you are fortunate enough to have any pre-production at all, it will consist of a script-reading (where the producers, director and leading actors all hate the script and go away to write their own versions), screen tests for costumes and make-up, horse-riding, dialect lessons and, if you are lucky, a few discussions with the director over a glass of wine. So, until you walk onto the set, you are your own director.

Of course, you will have a rehearsal on set before filming. This will vary enormously depending on the kind of production and kind of director. It often goes like this: you arrive on the set and the director introduces you, 'This is Mike – he is your husband. This is Caroline, playing your wife and this is the scene where you are having the row in the kitchen. Caroline, these are the plates you are going to throw…'!

If you are very lucky, your scene may get half an hour of your director's time. You need to use every moment to readjust to the new input and build relationships with the other actors. Then you will be sent off to make-up and costume and will have time to digest the new information before returning to the set to film it. If you are unlucky, you may enter a lit set with the camera already in place, be given precise instructions on how to move and say the lines and be filmed immediately: 'Now you kneel on this knee, and hold your hand out like this...'

A film director may never have worked with actors before. They may have come from animation, pop videos, special effects, editing, production or writing. You are only a small part of the filming process. The director chooses the crew for ability. If a director has not worked with actors before, they will simply expect them to play their parts well. They would not expect to help the Director of Photography set the lighting, the costume designer cut the fabric or the sound mixer balance the levels. So why should they think they need to help you with acting?

So, what do you do? How can you rehearse without finalised decisions? Well, to begin:

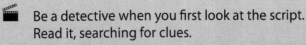 Be a detective when you first look at the script. Read it, searching for clues.

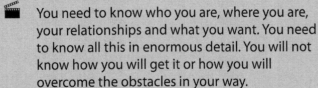 You need to know who you are, where you are, your relationships and what you want. You need to know all this in enormous detail. You will not know how you will get it or how you will overcome the obstacles in your way.

Make sure every place, person and object you refer to is as real to you as the people, places and things in your own life. If others in the scene know them too, it will help to share this knowledge when you meet and to choose references you all know.

 Use improvisation to fill in all the gaps in your knowledge and to fuel your needs. You can be imaginative and do it on your own, you can be extremely lucky and be able to do it with the actor with whom you are to play the scene, or you can use another partner. For example, if you are playing the elder of two adult sisters, then improvise bathing your younger sister's knee when she was ten. If you apologise to your friend for betraying the promise you made, then improvise that pledge you made ten years ago that you have now broken. If you have an injury that you mention in the scene, act out getting the injury.

 Find the physical life of the role. You will find detailed suggestions for this later in Workshop 3.

And the Other Differences...

In addition to the big three differences between stage and screen acting:

4. The Jigsaw

The bigger the budget, the more the filming will be broken up into bite-sized chunks. Each scene has lots of set-ups – a set-up being whenever the camera changes position. You have to keep re-finding the scene afresh each time. The tempo is completely different to the arc of theatre. In theatre, although you do the show again each night, you do it in its entirety. You don't have to enter a scene at the height of its intensity without the moment that triggers it coming first. And you don't have to keep repeating that section over and over again.

5. The Repetition

For each set-up, the scene or part of the scene is repeated for a number of takes. Again, the number will depend on the budget as well as the performance and the technical hitches. Each time must be as fresh and immediate as the first. You never know which take will be used. You can never do a take 'the same', you can only start from the same needs and thoughts and be in the moment again. You will have to stick to all the major moves you made, but subtle differences will and should be there. Remember that it has to be able to be cut together so continuity is important, but ultimately the film can only ever show one shot at a time, so the way you actually say a line does not have to match exactly.

6. Technical Demands

Filming makes more technical demands than theatre. You have to be able to hit your mark precisely without looking as if you are doing so, you have to bear continuity in mind, you can't bash your radio mic, you need to know what size shot you are in, you need to know how to think in the direction of the camera, and so on. But it is like driving a car. After all, you can drive your car and have a terrible row with your partner without knocking down any old ladies, and you can arrive at your destination without knowing how you got there, having negotiated all obstacles safely! In the same way, you can master all the techniques required for filming, practise until they are second nature, and then let your autopilot get on with them whilst you engage in the business of thought and communication.

7. Screen Reality

Not everything will feel 'organic' on film. You may declare love to a cameraman's hand or fight enemies represented by crosses on a green or blue backcloth. The camera distorts space, so you will often feel too close or at a strange angle to your partner. You have to trust the camera operator and director. If they say it looks right – it looks right.

8. It is Out of Your Hands

You do not have ultimate control over your performance. In the theatre, the director disappears on opening night. When you walk out on the stage, for better or worse, you call the shots. In film, not only does the director call the shots, but the resulting footage will be rearranged, cut, shaped, changed by computer-generated images and often dubbed. In short, everything except the moment that you are acting is out of your control. It is always part of the collaborative work to offer your creative thoughts and inspirations and to try to persuade the director into your way of thinking. But if you hit a blank wall, there is no point in fighting.

I have been on sets where actors have fought for control. Once I watched an actress, whose scene had been removed from the schedule, fight and fight for its reinstatement with a European director, who knew exactly the end result he wanted. Eventually he agreed but said to me when she left, 'We'll shoot it quickly but I'll cut it out of the film.' Which he did. In another film, I worked with an actor who felt he was being asked to make choices that felt unnatural. Eventually the script supervisor said in frustration, 'You can be organic if you want to but no one will see it.' And she was right. There is only one ultimate reality in this medium – what appears on the screen. And that, ultimately, is the film-maker's choice. Instead of fighting, use your energy to make your role alive and then the director may use more footage of you than you expected. Or even write a new scene!

9. It is Your Permanant Legacy

Unlike theatre, you cannot make up for a sticky beginning by being brilliant after the interval. You cannot keep adding to your performance to make it better every night. You cannot get away with being tired and bored one day and hoping no one will notice. It will end up on the digital cutting-room floor or be there for ever to haunt you.

10. It is the Last Travelling Circus

The days start really early and are really long. (It's an ironic fact that films hire the most beautiful people in the world, make them live for months on five hours' sleep a night and then have to hire the best and most expensive make-up and hair artists in the world to repair the damage!) You are often outside in really extreme conditions. You get lots of delicious free food if you are on location but are expected not to change shape. The crew, mysteriously (and unlike in the theatre), often seem to want the film or series to fail until it is shown and proves a hit. You have to keep your own faith and belief and walk away from negative gossip. Everything will take longer and you will be more bored waiting for your shot than you ever imagined, but when they need you they will need you faster than you can cope with. And the shot will be over quicker than you want.

I urge every actor and director to watch the first sequence in the film *Living in Oblivion* (1995), written and directed by Tom DiCillo. It really *is* like that!

Text – What Text?

Television was born from a heritage of words derived from theatre and radio and it has nurtured many wonderful writers. Thus, traditionally in television there has always been a proper script that has tended not to change too much and which directors have tended to respect. Television has to allow people to go and make a cup of tea or eat a meal whilst they watch, so there is quite a lot of dialogue to support the pictures and keep the plot running.

Film has evolved from silent movies and the picture rules. So many multimillion dollar movies go into production with half-formed scripts and there is often little respect for the form of the words, even if the script is well written. (That is why great screenwriters like Harold Pinter, David Mamet, Ingmar Bergman, Woody Allen and Anthony Minghella, for example, have so often ended up directing or producing their own work.) Screenplays change and change again and there are often so few words that it is hard for the actor to find many clues in the text. I worked with an actor on a film in a challenging role and we found a backstory and an attitude to the world based on the script. But when she started filming, the script was thrown away and she was left with moment-to-moment decisions as the cast improvised and the director changed each scene. It was an interesting endeavour – but text-based work it was not!

I suspect as television becomes more and more geared to the mass market it will move towards the way of film, and real text work will only be possible in a few worthy productions. So here are a few suggestions when you have little text to work with:

 Find your voice through the physical life of the role. If you have actual physical work to prepare, like horse-riding, sword-fighting, running, and so on, then speak your thoughts (as the role) out loud whilst you work. Use full voice to find the weight, measure, intonation, speed of thought and ease of speech that you need.

 Improvise moments from your past and speak them aloud. Get up in the morning as your role and vocalise your thoughts about the day ahead.

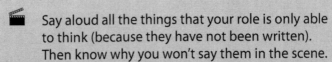

Say aloud all the things that your role is only able to think (because they have not been written). Then know why you won't say them in the scene.

If you are working in a different period or genre, then read aloud work of the period or a book about the situation to 'find your voice'. So you might use Shakespeare or Austen, Hemingway or Chandler depending on the context of the piece. Find poetry that inspires you or describe your imagined scenery or clothes or the day itself to a long-suffering friend or into your camcorder.

The lack of text can bring its own rewards. The producer Norman Jewison tells the story of Steve McQueen in *The Thomas Crown Affair* (1968). Whilst other actors wanted more lines, Steve always asked to have his dialogue cut. Jewison had to urge him to keep some so that the performance wasn't built solely on reaction shots. Of course, the finished product was a legendary performance and when we think of Steve McQueen, we think of that still electrifying presence. He was right, of course. When someone is speaking at length, what we want to see is how the words are being received. So in the end, with film, picture does rule!

Big and Small?

When actors are not properly connected and working from their core, they start to push and their faces move more. They drive the words and not the thought. Then the director, often not able to help with acting problems, desperately tries to make the actor look more human. 'Do it smaller,' he or she will wail or 'Do less,' or, possibly more helpfully, 'Stop acting!'

I constantly observe actors being wonderful in rehearsal, but when 'Action!' is called, they feel obliged to consciously 'add' something to make us understand the subtext. I once watched a very experienced actor do a wonderful camera rehearsal but, on the first take, he started to 'act'. He said later that, before the camera turned, he had simply been talking to the others in the scene without 'doing' anything. The director and I had seen that this first rehearsal had actually been much more compelling and truthful than the subsequent takes.

Because we are afraid of being boring, we want to add things to our performance to make it more interesting. In his auto-biography, *The Magic Lantern*, the legendary film director Ingmar Bergman talks about working with Ingrid Bergman, late in her life, when she was very ill. Because she had lost confidence in herself, she apparently came to set with her part all worked out and Ingmar wanted her to strip it back down to play it truthfully. He remarks, 'I asked her a hundred times not to do anything at all and that only bloody amateurs think they have to do something every single moment.' It is a harsh remark about a good actor, but one worth remembering. You need only to do what you would need to do – no more.

Jack Lemmon used to tell the story of his first film, directed by George Cukor. He said he received the best acting advice he was ever given. After 'Take one', Cukor took him to one side and said, 'Very good, Jack. But can you make it a bit smaller?' After 'Take two': 'Excellent, Jack. But a bit less.' After 'Take three': 'You've nearly got it but even less.' 'Take four': the same. After 'Take five', Jack said, 'If I do anything less, I won't be doing anything at all.' George Cukor replied, 'Now you got it!'

What Cukor really meant was 'Stop acting'. Because truthful reaction isn't necessarily small but you can't add anything untruthful. And in spite of that advice, Jack Lemmon never held himself back but went on to do work which, at its best, is remarkably truthful and funny. His role as the musician who gets into drag to escape the Mafia in Billy Wilder's *Some Like it Hot* (1959) is still one of the funniest performances on celluloid. But, within the extremity of the situation and the needs of his role, the performance is founded on truth – that is why we laugh so much.

This 'being' in the moment of the given situation, without signalling to an imaginary audience, preparing how to say the lines or adding tension because of your own embarrassment or nerves is what I believe is meant by that old axiom in film of 'less is more'. I do not believe that theatre is 'big' or film is 'small'. 🎞 **1.6**

Of course, in theatre, there is that (relatively) distant audience and you have to make sure they can understand what you feel. You don't have that problem on camera, but film can't be smaller than life. On the contrary, your reactions are likely to be (truthfully) enormous. Films are usually about high emotions or extreme situations, and deal with the wilder side of life. If you think of great actors – Marlon Brando, Robert De Niro, Bette Davis, Katharine Hepburn, Anthony Hopkins, Philip Seymour Hoffman and, indeed, Jack Lemmon – you could never call their performances 'small'. They are intense, funny and vivid. They are driven by high stakes and pursue strong objectives.

If you were unlucky enough to have something ghastly happen to you in life, and there were a camera running on you at the time, no one could ever accuse you of being 'too big'. You would simply be real. If you were videoing your children's birthday party when the pilot bailed out of a passing plane and fell through the ceiling, would anyone say the reactions of the guests were 'too big' when they played the footage on the evening news?

When you catch on camera a child or a cat or someone who doesn't get camera-shy, engaged in what they happen to be doing – they look wonderful. You don't say to the cat, 'You must make your movements smaller – don't wave your paws around like that!'

Human beings engaged in pursuit of their needs and drives are naturally rooted and truthful, and can be enormous. But the unnatural business of using someone else's words, the technical requirements of film, and the need to please can result in the actor blocking off from this centre and consequently a diminution of the performance. So, far from being minimalist, you will usually have to go further to encompass the extremity of the situation you are playing. I believe that in the big/small debate, we are actually talking about whether an actor is 'connected' or 'disconnected'. If the actor is working from their centre or core, the work will be perceived as truthful and everything will be free and feel effortless.

In life, when we are 'connected up' emotionally, we speak from our abdominal-diaphragmatic area without even being aware of it. When actors are on stage, the very act of engaging with an audience and communicating through a projected voice by using those abdominal muscles means the actor is automatically emotionally centred too. But, on screen, there is usually no need for any kind of vocal projection to centre the actor, and, because it is not life, the actor is not automatically connected up. Because there is no audience to take our attention outwards and we are not really engaging with the others in the scene, we move into ourselves, 'thinking' about our feelings and trying to 'do well'.

Thus, screen acting can be the most dangerous medium of all for the actor who is neither connected to the abdominal-diaphragmatic area by 'life' or by a necessary automatic stage technique. Without engaging this area, the actor also becomes disconnected from the need that is driving the role and disconnected from the emotional, vocal and energy 'centre'. Then you see manufactured emotion, frowning, the face moving too much and the performance seems too 'big'.

If you look around, you will notice that even when emotional or stressed, people's brows are generally smooth. They don't frown that much and their eyes rarely screw up (except when they smile), however animated they get. Actors, on the other hand, often push their words, frown and screw up their eyes to convince themselves they are 'feeling'!

The camera teaches you to be clear and specific. Emily Watson said, 'I think I only began to understand acting when I went into film. It is such precise work; the emotional planet is very clear.'

Film is not about doing less – it is simply that it is a microscope and will show falseness and 'manufactured' emotions that are not truly rooted in the actor. It is about less bad acting – not less life! You can be truthful and enormous – if your role's reactions to life are enormous! 💿 **1.6** (Steve's character is in court and therefore playing to an audience within the world of the drama. That is not the same as stepping outside the world of the script and 'showing' the viewers.)

💿 **Now watch the Introduction and Workshop 1 on the DVD.**

Workshop 2

Inhabiting the Role

Workshop
2

The Power of the Lens

A camera acts like a microscope, it magnifies everything. Martin Scorsese calls it 'the psychic strength of the lens'. Let me remind you again - it sees you think. It can't tell what you are thinking, but you have to trust that it does see you think. Which means you don't have to do the extra work of showing us what you are thinking. If you do that, you will be 'acting' and we will not believe you.

When you are next on a train or a bus, look at the people around you. Put the person opposite you into an imaginary close-up. Imagine the situation they are in: they could be at their father's graveside, or their best friend's marriage to their ex-girlfriend, or their first job interview. That is how they would look. Their thoughts would be private, but they would be alive and thinking.

That is why it is possible to steal a close-up from a film and then to transplant it into another film with a different scenario and yet the viewer will still be able to believe it to be consistent with the plot. The Soviet filmmaker Lev Kuleshov did experiments in the early part of the twentieth century to show that the juxtaposition of shots influence viewers' reactions. For example, if you cut to a close-up of an actor's face and then to a bowl of soup – people will claim to have seen hunger in the actor's eyes.

Alfred Hitchcock once gave a vivid example of this. He showed a close-up of himself looking serious, then cut to a mother and baby then cut once more to himself in close-up, smiling. He explained that the viewer would then receive his image as a benign, elderly gentleman who liked babies. He then recut it, replacing the mother and baby with a shot of a girl sunbathing in a skimpy bikini. The resulting reaction to Hitchcock's smiling close-up would then be 'Dirty old man!'

You don't want to be doing the work of the writer, director and editor. They will tell the story through the script and the shots. If you try to do it for them by 'showing' us, you will simply be fake. 💿 **1.5**

Close-Up and Personal

❝ The close-up says everything. It's then that an actor's learned, rehearsed behaviour becomes most obvious to an audience and chips away, unconsciously, at its experience of reality. In close-up, the audience is only inches away, and your face becomes the stage.

Marlon Brando

On screen, you need to be responding truthfully within your imaginary world. You need to be thinking and alive in every moment. But with your 'stage-manager head', it is important to know what shot you are in. 💿 **4.6** Your parameter of movement may be small and you need to discuss this with the camera operator. In a really tight close-up, even shifting your weight from one foot to the other can be enough to put you out of focus.

There may be other technical requirements like holding a prop higher so that it can be seen or not waving your hands up and down in front of your face. When you speak dialogue, you need to be careful not to overlap with the actor who is giving you lines off screen so that it can be edited easily later. Be kind to the hair and make-up department. If a hair is blowing in front of your nostrils, it is all we will focus on, so allow them to do their work – they are making sure we watch you properly.

By the way, some jargon you may hear: a 'clean single' is when only you are in the close-up, a 'dirty' close-up (not as exciting as it sounds) simply means there will be a part of another person's face, hair or body also in the close-up with you. 💿 4.6

But is there a different acting style for close-ups? It's a question I am often asked and no, I don't think so. Having said that, though, you are going to be seen really close up in a 'close-up'. On a large screen, every nervous twitch and grimace will look enormous. So your breathing and centring work will become crucial to stop you swaying in the frame or showing any tension on the face. If you are 'showing' or not reacting 'in the moment', the camera will see any falseness clearly. But you should be doing that in all your work anyway!

The only other thing to remember is that if your gestures were revealing what you wanted and how you were reacting in the master shot, they will not be seen in close-up – we have to understand those needs through your eyes and voice. If you take your gaze somewhere near the camera, we will see your thoughts better than if you are looking down or to your side.

There is an ancient Greek proverb, which Buster Keaton used in explanation of his marvellous comedy work, 'Act fast, think slowly.' But if I have any tip for close-up work, it is to turn that on its head and 'Think fast, act slowly.' By that

I mean your mind should be alive with thought, taking in all the teeming possibilities, reacting to outside stimulus, searching your mind for solutions, but your actual movements should be calm and easy.

■ You need to be actually listening, as if for the first time, being aware of your environment and watching to see the effect of your words and actions. You need to give yourself time to hear and think. Close-ups are about receiving from the other characters and the situation. 📀 **1.2**

■ If it does not interfere with how you stood in the master shot, you can rest your hand on your stomach when you play an emotional scene. This will help you access your emotions and feel connected. It will stop you 'pushing' and jutting your chin forward, because if you do that, you will lose power and status (as well as looking less than great!). 📀 **3.2.a, 4.3**

■ If you are sitting and it matches the master shot, ground yourself by resting your feet firmly on the floor. Be careful that you are not tapping or wriggling your feet as you will 'leak out' energy and you may bob up and down within the frame. 📀 **4.3, 4.4**

■ Don't feel that you have to look at the other character all the time. In life, unless we are persuading or bullying or pleading or consoling, we are unlikely to hold a steady gaze. We interact with our surroundings, and things happening around us impinge on us and take our attention. Every time we have a new thought or picture in our head or are dealing with our feelings, we look away. The stronger your relationship is, the less likely you are to hold a gaze. You can tell who is on a first date and who has been married ten years if you look at couples in a restaurant. The married couple may hardly make eye contact! 💿 **2.6, 4.1**

 If you have to look deeply into someone's eyes and they are only a foot away, we will see your gaze flickering from one of their eyes to the other. This might look good in wider shots especially if you are excited or exhilarated. But if you are in a tight close-up, especially in semi-profile, this darting gaze can be distracting and you will lose the strength of the performance. So favour the eye of your partner that is nearest to the camera. Then we will see your eyes better and you will look more focused. I say 'favour' because unless you intend the gaze to be really firm – for example, because you are trying to extract some information from someone or won't let them off the hook – a totally fixed look will make your eyes start to look 'dead'. 💿 **4.1**

Generally, extreme close-ups will only be used for still moments, where you are thinking or reacting. But on many films, these days, they use a moving camera, which follows you around in close-up, whilst another camera catches a wider view. In this case, my advice would be to forget the framing and just to act the scene, thinking hard and staying focused. When the film is edited, the director will then choose the close-up moments that the camera has caught.

The Eyes Have It

Your eyes, truly, light up when you think. Just mentioning someone you love produces a momentary, but unmistakable, gleam in your eye. 💿 **2.1**

Film actors have always known this and some of the famous Hollywood stars of the 1940s used to demand, in their contracts, their own 'key-light' to add light to their eyes. Calling the eyes 'the windows of your soul' has become a cliché for a good reason – through them we can see that you are alive with thoughts and feelings and existing in this precise moment of time.

As I've said before, so often when actors are on text, the life seems to drain out of their eyes. 💿 **1.3** The little crinkles of amusement, irony or warmth seem to instantly iron out. This is another tip for 'Star Quality' – keep that life in your eyes – if you are charming someone, keep that charm; if you are flirting, keep your sexuality; if you are interested, keep your attitude to what you are hearing. Keep your intelligence, keep your subtext, keep your life.

George Clooney is a supreme example of an actor who keeps his inner life showing at the corners of his eyes. Jeff Bridges is another. Think of Spencer Tracy, Denzel Washington, Jack Nicholson, Donald Sutherland, Kristin Scott Thomas, Judi Dench, Charlotte Rampling, Julia Roberts, Angelina Jolie or Carey Mulligan and you think of how their eyes light up to show you what they think or to reveal their subtext. Watch Humphrey Bogart and Katharine Hepburn battle it out in *The African Queen* (1951)! These are some of the examples that have sprung immediately to mind, but there are very few really great film actors that wouldn't share this trait. So:

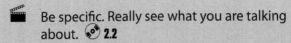

🎬 Be specific. Really see what you are talking about. 💿 **2.2**

🎬 If you haven't time to create imaginary people that you can invest with real attributes – use people you do know. If you and the other actor or actors share the knowledge of this person, choose someone you all know. 🎬 **2.5**

Keep thinking. Don't go dead whilst waiting for your next line. 💿 **1.1, 1.5, 4.1**

Keep listening. You don't know what will be said next. You don't know how it will turn out. You don't know what action you will take. As each obstacle comes up, you deal with it at that moment. *You don't know what will happen next.* 💿 **1.1, 1.3**

Keep seeing the outer world around you. Deal with things and activities as you would need to in life to get the job done. 💿 **2.6**

Watch your partner like a hawk (whether overtly or circumspectly will depend on the scene) – see how your words and actions are affecting them.

Don't screw your eyes up or frown too much – sure signs that you are 'acting'. 💿 **1.4, 1.5, 2.1**

Keep the humour and intelligence in your eyes. Keep a view of the world and a response to it. The role will always be 'you' at the core – with the particulars of the role you have worked on. So keep life in your eyes. 💿 **1.1, 2.0, 2.1**

Remember – nobody is one-dimensional. We all carry baggage and attitudes and our unique take on life, whatever situation we are in. The role must be as least as interesting and complex as you are. 💿 **1.3, 1.4, 2.1, 2.3**

Thoughts and Wants

The camera sees when you have needs and feelings. **2.0, 2.1, 3.9** Sometimes the most extraordinary moments happen on screen when the actor forgets the lines! In that moment, their eyes are alight and they appear to be grappling with some enormous emotional conflict. Unfortunately, the actor rarely remembers the line to continue the scene. Instead, the plaintive 'I've dried…' or the expletive breaks the spell.

We can tell when the stakes are high. We may not know what they are but we can see the person thinking – hard. And we can see those wheels turning violently whilst the actor struggles to find the words.

It is extraordinary how remembering the lines seems to be more important than what is going on in the circumstances of the scene. The needs and actions that drive you in the role have to be as strong as they would be in actuality. Your imagination has to engage with the situation 'as if' it is really happening to you. The camera will see your eyes go dead if your imaginary world is not as specific and as involving as the real world. And surely there is more at stake in the scene than whether or not you know your lines!

You can never go on to autopilot. If you are waiting for your line or lose focus with the scene, we will see the light go out of your eyes. At the very least, engage with the real world around you – really look at the other actors, the props, the set – and listen!

> Know what you want and speak it out loud before you go on set. Think it again before the camera turns.

If you are really listening and watching the other characters and the environment (real or imagined) and dealing with the situation to get what you need, your thoughts will keep whirring.

The Picture in Your Head

Most of us are very visual. As we speak, pictures pop into our mind's eye (and you can actually see people's eyes flicking up to these pictures **1.1, 2.1, 2.2, 2.3**). Because the world you inhabit has to be created by your imagination, the words aren't your own and the scene has to be repeated over and over again, it is crucial to create these pictures and keep them flashing up. If you've done your homework well, you won't have to try to do this, it will happen of its own accord.

But if you are not in the moment of what you are saying or doing, you will lose connection to these visual memories. You may be someone who hears or tastes or smells your memories instead. In that case, you must keep these senses working in your imaginary world.

 Tell someone where you are going tonight or what you were doing last weekend. Did you have pictures or some other internal memory flash up?

Once you have become aware of these flashes of memory, make sure they also happen to you in your role.

Letting the Words Fall Out

In life, we often stand relaxed, leaning against a wall, quietly thinking and then words arise out of us with no effort. Yet, on screen, I see so many actors in close-up who start the scene looking wonderful, their eyes alive with thought. I want nothing to change except words to form out of these thoughts. Instead, as the line arises in the actor's head, I see the life drain out of their eyes – they move slightly – tense their necks – shift forward – and then 'say' the line. 📀 **1.3**

Words on a page are simply hieroglyphics for thoughts – thoughts that are either being revealed through the words or hidden behind them. You have to think hard and allow the thoughts to fall out. Or maybe they need to be pulled out like teeth. The words become the physical manifestation of the thought, the picture in your head, the need. They have to arise, unbidden.

When Vanessa Redgrave received the BAFTA Fellowship Award in 2010 at the Royal Opera House, she credited her most valuable acting advice to watching the opera singer Maria Callas there. She said she realised that 'you have to put the truth of your feelings and your thoughts first, and the sound of your voice would and could come after'.

As we've seen, the camera can go in close enough to read how you feel through your eyes. 📀 **1.5** Film capitalises on this and screen dialogue is pretty sparse. Whereas Othello finds verse line after verse line of metaphors to describe jealousy, a film character might simply grit his teeth and say, 'Pour me another whisky.'

To remind yourself how words can happen without you showing any decisions to speak:

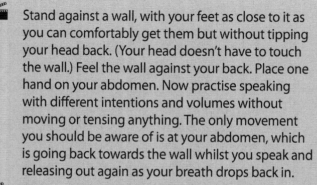

Stand against a wall, with your feet as close to it as you can comfortably get them but without tipping your head back. (Your head doesn't have to touch the wall.) Feel the wall against your back. Place one hand on your abdomen. Now practise speaking with different intentions and volumes without moving or tensing anything. The only movement you should be aware of is at your abdomen, which is going back towards the wall whilst you speak and releasing out again as your breath drops back in.

Stand back to back with a friend. Imagine you are sending the sound through your back to your partner. Speak loudly at first so they can hear clearly and then very quietly so they feel only vibration through their back.

Lie relaxed and heavy on the floor and then speak aloud. Again, you should feel only the gentle downward pressure of your stomach muscles and a gentle vibration in your throat, back and chest as you speak, followed by the upward release of your abdomen at the end of the thought. No other part of you should be tensing or lifting off the floor.

Sometimes you will want to use strong muscularity of speech in order to get what you want. And you will be aware of using it. Try this improvisation:

You are on your mobile phone talking to someone you love, trying to get them to do something they don't want to do. Or you are telling them off for something they didn't do. There are people around and you don't want them to hear the conversation.

What did you notice? You almost certainly didn't whisper because that doesn't work on mobile phones. (And you shouldn't whisper in intimate scenes on camera – you need a little 'tone' to your voice – see Workshop 4: 'Sound'.) You probably used a low private tone with a flat urgent 'tune' and strong consonants to reinforce what you were saying. And if the listener didn't understand you or didn't agree to do what you wanted then you probably, instinctively, increased the strength of your consonants.

When we are not in subtext and we're using the words to communicate our needs, they will have enormous energy and importance. The need to speak them has to be as strong as it would be in life, otherwise you will iron out the energy and the words will be flat and lifeless and not carry the meaning. But this strength will come from the strength of thought.

For example, we don't tail away in life if we want someone to understand or to do something – we drive to the end of the thought because if we don't, we won't get what we want: 'Pass me the *eggs*. And the *butter*.'

If you tail away on 'eggs' and 'butter', you are not in the moment of that thought. You have jumped to the next one – because you know the lines. While I'm thinking about eggs, I'm not yet worried about butter!

It's 'eggs' and 'butter' that carry the natural stress. Those are the words you will hit, as those are the things you want. Don't get caught up in unimportant words. Hit these important ones, and just travel through the rest. Otherwise, the other person won't get the point!

We have become shy of being eloquent and using rich language. Actors often try to use a 'naturalistic style' when working with heightened text in period films. This is not related to why they are speaking or the lives they lead. Even in their everyday lives, these same actors would have so much more energy in their speech as they 'found' each specific word to communicate what was important to them. If your role uses wit or enjoys language, you too must enjoy the language you use. And the language will fit with the situation, setting and role.

When Stanley Kubrick asked Kirk Douglas for more diction on the film *Spartacus* (1960), Kirk is famously reputed to have said, 'Diction? If I had any diction, I'd still be a bum on Broadway.'

And, behind this light-hearted remark is the truth that how you speak is tied up with who and where you are. You cannot 'say lines' on screen. You can't concentrate on 'how' to say them. (Even if you are working on a dialect you have to link it with the life of the role.) You speak as you in the role would *need* to speak.

With his gravelly voice and strong physicality, Kirk Douglas was true to the role he was playing as a man of action, not words, uneducated and unused to speaking in public, driven by physicality and passion rather than eloquence. The words have to come from who you are and what you want. You will only need 'diction' if you in the role need to make yourself understood or it is true to the role you are playing.

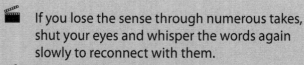

- If you lose the sense through numerous takes, shut your eyes and whisper the words again slowly to reconnect with them.

- If the words are unusual, complicated, descriptive or poetic, act them out with gestures when you prepare.

- Then, having made them your own, just let them happen as you think the thought.

And have one thought at a time. Don't run sentences together. In life, we take a breath on each new thought and when the writer puts a full stop, it means a new thought. So dare not to know what you will say next. Stop at the end of the thought. Then let the next come to you. Or if a new thought comes to you whilst you are still speaking, know exactly where that thought supplants the last one. Different roles will have different rhythms of speech, and actors are usually more even in their rhythms than we ever are in life. In life, words suddenly explode out of us. Or dry up altogether.

Have the courage to drive the words. Don't let the words drive you. Give yourself permission to feel that it is really you talking and to take the time to mint the words as you go. They must come out fresh in the moment. That doesn't mean you need to say them slowly, there may be times that you drive them at great speed, but they can't come out on autopilot. They must be connected up with you, just like life. There are no rules; they may bubble out of you, cut through the air or fall like stones – but however they emerge, they are *your* words – you 'as if'.

Connecting Up with the Script

There will, of course, be scripted dialogue in films and more in television. And you could find yourself with a really wonderful script by Tom Stoppard, Sam Shepard, Martin McDonagh, Aaron Sorkin, Charlie Kaufman or Sofia Coppola. In every crop of films nominated for the awards each year, there will always be a few with sparkling scripts. Not all actors know how to do them justice.

Recently, writing to an acting teacher, I was trying to pinpoint why dealing with text is so difficult and why, when actors read lines, they become lighter, less engaged and less powerful than they are in life. As we've seen, working from a given text is an unnatural act. We never speak or move in life in a conscious manner without an impulse or thought directing us to do so.

Sanford Meisner famously said, 'Text is your greatest enemy.' What is being asked of an actor is that they have a real impulse that comes up and gives rise in that split second of time to the only words that will precisely serve that need and those happen to be the words that are printed on the page!

When you need something or want to communicate, the brain fires up and, almost simultaneously, so does the area around the 'solar plexus' – the abdominal-diaphragmatic region. The inspiration of breath that fills our lungs by the contraction of the diaphragm is also the breath that we take in with the inspiration of the thought.

This breath connection gets disrupted because the words on the page are not our own spontaneous thoughts. If you are drawing a high tense breath into your upper chest in order to prepare or letting the breath out before you speak, this is a sure sign that you have disengaged from the words and that this link between thought and breath has become disconnected. 🎧 **2.4**

In life, we dig around for the words to match the pictures in our head that we want to communicate and, out of this need, words arrive and either fall out or have to be dredged up depending on the need and strength of emotion.

When actors look at a text, the words are a given on the page. So the only want or need that spontaneously arrives is simply the need to decipher them, to decode them. An actor has to get beyond this decoding mode, which allows words to fly out on autopilot with no weight or connection to self, to get behind the real and specific need that drives them. You will often see a furrowed brow appear as the actor deals with the printed words that are being remembered. The director

Penny Cherns says that we frown because it is as if we 'read' the words off the front of our brains.

If I use the imagistic idea of centres of energy – the 'head centre' is where we deal with logic and reasoning. You are in your head centre when you are decoding the printed word on the page. So when we read or remember the words themselves, it is as if they come solely from the head and don't connect to the abdominal area, where we 'feel'. We have to absorb what is behind those words and then reroute the text so that instead of coming 'down' from the brain, it feels as if it comes 'up' from the solar plexus with the impulses. This is our lifetime's work.

This head-routing explains the actor's desire to push the head forward, go off centre, be too light, be too fast, let the words run away with themselves, 'colour' the words with false emotion, stand outside of them and 'explain them', get pushed, get 'patterned' and all the other problems we know only too well. This is because we know what we are going to say, we are not newly minting the language in the moment of impulse – the words cost us nothing.

Having explored the needs, images and reasons to speak the lines during rehearsal, you then have to bury them back into your subconscious. Then when the need arises, those words simply arise – easily or painfully.

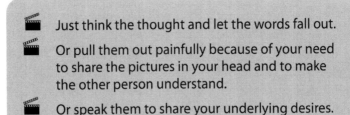

Just think the thought and let the words fall out.

Or pull them out painfully because of your need to share the pictures in your head and to make the other person understand.

Or speak them to share your underlying desires.

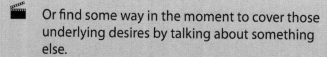 Or find some way in the moment to cover those underlying desires by talking about something else.

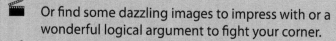 Or find some dazzling images to impress with or a wonderful logical argument to fight your corner.

Or find any other reason that drives you to speak.

But you cannot see the lines as an end in themselves; they only exist because of what gives rise to them.

Learning to Unlearn

All actor training, whether it is the work of Stanislavsky, Strasberg or Meisner, is about making the text come alive, so that these given words arrive as our own spontaneous thoughts and needs. Some theatre companies have even tried never looking at the text directly on the page during rehearsal, but having the actors tell each other the words they are to speak.

Marlon Brando, in his late films, used to wear an ear piece and have the text relayed to him through it so that he didn't have the disconnection of having to learn it. At least that is why he said that he did it! And it is true that learning lines means that you may get set into patterns. You have to learn the lines and then allow your conscious brain to forget them. You have to trust they'll pop out at the right moment!

In order to do this you have to learn lines really well, but learn them in such a way that you don't get patterned and you are able to change them if they get rewritten:

- Find the reason why you speak and what you want.

- Know your relationship with the other character.

- Work out how one thought needs to the next.

- Give yourself mental pictures of everything you talk about.

- If there is subtext, uncover what is underneath by speaking your unspoken thoughts aloud.

- If you find it a difficult text or it's from a different period, paraphrase it in idiomatic modern language, then return to the original words.

- If the script is not in your first language, paraphrase it in your native language first to connect with the words at the deepest level possible. Our first language is born organically out of desires and needs. The second language that we learn, even as a child, enters primarily through our cognitive faculties, through learning and decoding even if we connect up with it at a deeper level later. When you return to the language you are to work with, keep any new intensity or depth you have found.

- Now learn it. Acting it out may fix it by a process of osmosis, but you will probably have to resort to covering the words with a ruler to make it accurate.

- Some people find writing it out with the hand they don't normally use is helpful – left hand for right-handed or right for left-handed people.

- Try drawing pictures that connect you to your lines whilst you learn them.

- Practise the words doing lots of different activities: singing, chanting, jumping, doing the washing-up, in the bath, half-asleep, doing the gardening, walking the dog or speaking like an automaton. This is to avoid getting into a patterned rhythm and fixing how to 'say' them.

 When you almost know them, write them down and compare your writing with the original text. What have you substituted or got wrong? Find the specific link or need that leads you back to the original words.

A good test is whether you can dip in and out of the lines. If I say to an actor, 'Pick it up from…' and they have to go four lines back to get there, I know they are 'patterned'. A half-learned script makes your life very difficult, as your primary impulse will be to remember the words.

During production, however, the script is often changed or added to at the last minute. Sometimes a whole new scene appears minutes before filming. (Film is worse than television for this.) When that happens, don't panic. You will find you can hold new text in your short-term memory and even improvise it a little. Some film actors like to work this way in any case because they distrust their ability to stay fresh if they have learnt the script. To do this well, they still have to learn every beat of thought. I don't recommend this approach, but if there is no time to learn it properly, at least know how one thought leads to the next.

The text does not stand alone. Everything is linked. Breath, thought, words and movement cannot be separated. The mind and the body, voice and movement, imagination and memory are all connected up and are all involved in the act of communication. And they are all driven by our impulses.

In my experience, the actors who don't learn their lines at all need ten takes to look spontaneous. When they do achieve it, it's because they've learnt them by then anyway. Actors who are theatre trained or respect good scripts know that if you learn text deeply it enhances, rather than hinders, spontaneity.

Emotional Truth

So much of our work as actors is about emotion. In our roles, we tell stories about our traumatic pasts, we live through unbearable suffering, and deal with situations the like of which we hope we will never encounter in our own lives. Films are cathartic. Through the power of fiction, human beings explore the fears and horrors in their imaginations that they hope they will never be called upon to deal with in reality.

Actors are caring, responsible people who, by definition, empathise with the roles they play and want to do well in embodying them. So they tend to fall into a couple of traps. Either they stand outside the role and show us how terrible or how sad the situation is by 'signalling' to us what we should feel. Or, they are sending their attention into themselves instead of sending it out through their actions. They want to 'feel'. A very common request that I get from actors is to help them to cry and to let their emotions flow.

This is understandable, and when I was an actor I also wanted to be able to cry on cue. And there are some techniques to help, like triggers, that you will find detailed later in Workshop 3. But in life we rarely give in to our feelings and cry intentionally unless we are using it to block out the world around or simply letting go as a kind of personal therapy. Instead, we fight the tears so that they don't get in the way of the task in hand.

Actors strive to get a kinaesthetic feedback that they are 'feeling' and therefore working truthfully. But in life, there is no such feedback. Actors who are 'in the moment' report that the work feels effortless. Sometimes this worries them because they feel they are not 'working'. But when they watch the results, they see that more is actually happening. An actor wrote to me, after some work together:

> ❝ The strangest feeling was that I felt I wasn't 'doing' anything and was a total fraud! By this, I mean that work and a certain work ethic is associated with actually doing something or at least to have been seen to do something (the desire to please) and, by not actively expressing the 'doing', I was actually cheating, not doing my job!! Once I had realised this and managed to allow myself not to 'work', the results were better.

Associated with this need to 'work' is that desire to stand outside the role and show us, the viewer, either how the character is feeling or how we should feel about the character. So the text is 'coloured' with an emotional overlay, whereas in life people are usually very matter-of-fact until the moment that the emotion overwhelms them.

(❂ **2.7** Look how matter of fact the speakers are when they are talking about emotional events. Sometimes they even smile or laugh. ❂ **2.8** When I asked Candy to do this with her text, she became even more moving.)

I was lucky enough to see Vanessa Redgrave at the National Theatre in the play *The Year of Magical Thinking*, based on Joan Didion's account of the loss of her husband and daughter. It was an object lesson in dealing with difficult emotional material. Vanessa was truthful and even funny whilst talking of her grief. And the rare moments when the pain overwhelmed her were doubly moving because of her brave efforts to control the tears. We are moved more by bravery to deal with pain than tears themselves and tend to recoil from people who feel sorry for themselves – however deservedly.

In life, we try to get on with the business in hand – pursuing our needs by taking action and dealing with the emotion as it comes up, in order to continue with the task. If you are telling the police where you last saw your loved one, you will fight your tears to give them the information. If tears well up when you are defending yourself against a false allegation, you will angrily brush your tears away, wishing they were not getting in your way. If you have to tell someone bad news, you will be careful not to upset them, even though you are hurting inside. It is this bravery which moves us. 🎧 **2.8** (I asked Fernando to hide his emotion so as not to upset everyone at the funeral and I think his bravery is more compelling than when he gives in to his emotion.)

It is the hiding of emotion that becomes emotional for an audience. The classic British film *Brief Encounter* (1945) is a perfect example of raging emotions hiding behind tweedy post-war British breasts and stiff upper lips. When Celia Johnson's good and brave husband implies that he knows that she has been wrestling with her feelings for someone else and says, 'You've been a long way away. Thank you for coming back to me,' we cry as Rachmaninov provides the subtext.

In *A Single Man* (2009), Colin Firth takes a phone call about his lover's death. He tries to take in the terrible news and the realisation that he is not wanted at the funeral, whilst at the same time trying to maintain a social politeness. It is a master-class in how to have a maelstrom happening within whilst your brain takes in lots of new, unbearable information and you deal only with the conscious moment of interaction on the surface.

If you think about films that make you cry, you will find it is not usually about the sadness of the characters or the situation. It is the bravery with which the situation is dealt with or the moment when emotion breaks through of its own accord after it has been held in check. For example, when two people fight their emotions for a long time and then finally hold each other and are overwhelmed by their feelings, then we cry too as a cathartic release.

If we tell a story of something terrible that happened to us, we move between seeing the pictures of the events in our mind's eye and the physical feelings that the memories evoke, and the act of telling the other person – trying to get them to share these pictures in our head. In the course of this, we will often act surprisingly – laughing at the worst moments, for example. And as we recount the awful things that have happened, we will, as we saw, sound surprisingly matter-of-fact. 💿 **2.7**

Our emotions lie suppressed within us like molten lava, which occasionally bubbles up and, just sometimes, overwhelms us. We seldom *try* to feel and yet that is what most actors do most of the time. We strive to be light, unemotional, not to distress the onlooker and not to distress ourselves by going too far back into our disturbing memories. If we allowed ourselves to go completely into that painful past, we couldn't cope with the present. So we generally try to avoid it. You will often see people talking about a painful memory patting their upper chest with an open hand as if they are actually pushing the emotion back down so as not to deal with it at that moment.

You have to do all the homework of understanding the facts and the horrors and improvising the past, finding the 'triggers' and using whatever works to put that molten lava in place. Then you just trust that it lies there buried whilst you get on with the task in hand – and let the emotion take care of itself. If it erupts of its own accord like a volcano, you deal with it! 💿 **2.8**

Finding the Core

" By degrees we reach the innermost depths, which we define as the core, the mysterious 'I'. That is where human emotions exist in their pristine stage; there in the fiery furnace of human passions all that is trivial, shallow, is consumed, only the fundamental organic elements of an actor's creative nature remain.

Constantin Stanislavsky
Creating a Role

As we saw in Workshop 1, really good actors do seem to offer a window into the essential core of their being. With each part they play, they twist the viewpoint so that they are believable in many different roles. And yet the essential essence of themselves remains constant.

No matter what part they play and how different their role's background, appearance or view of the world, there is always a constant unchanging part of themselves that is there in the performance. They can play deep and serious or trivial and shallow people, because they understand what it would be like to be that person. For the time that they embody the writer's creation, they joyfully play the game of really being 'as if' in those shoes. The characters they play are not separate puppets held up for our entertainment, they are living creatures grounded in the actors themselves.

It seems too simple to suggest that this grounding is governed by the breath and the impulses that arrive from the 'centre', that mysterious area around the solar plexus that we instinctively feel is the seat of our emotional life. But the more I work with actors, the more I feel that this 'core' we strive for has a very physical basis and that rooting the breath in this abdominal-diaphragmatic area – and driving the impulses from there – does release the actor in a very deep way.

Breathing Life into the Role

You take your first breath in as you enter the world and let your last breath out as you leave it. Just as the word 'inspire' means both to breathe in and to energise through thought and feeling, so 'expire' means both to die and to breathe out. The moral of this is that breathing is essential to life! When you are on screen, we need to believe in the life of your role, a living, breathing life. If you tense up and stop breathing while you take in new information, the life will go out of the moment. We will see the lack of thought behind your eyes. Thinking, listening and reacting in the moment are essential ingredients for film acting, and it is hard to think or listen when you are holding your breath. Lines will be forgotten and connection with other characters will be lost. (And so will any control over continuity or hitting the mark!)

If you see someone on screen talking about something that excites them, their eyes will dance and sparkle. They will become 'lit up' from within. 💿 **2.1** Each new thought they take will be accompanied by a new breath which brings the text to vivid, exciting life. And it will keep the actor vivid and alive too. (But more, much more of this in Workshop 3!)

Recipe for STAR Quality

On a lighter note, I've come up with my recipe for success:

> **S**it or stand up straight
> **T**hink
> **A**nd
> **R**emember to breathe! 💿 **3.2**

It sounds deceptively simple, doesn't it? But I think it merits some unpicking. Thought and breath are so linked that they are almost indivisible. In some recent research, it was shown by ultrasound scans that as soon as you have an impulse to speak or move, the area around the diaphragm responds almost simultaneously.

This area round the diaphragm is also where you 'feel'. If your energy comes from there, your impulses will be rooted in truth. Stanislavsky talked of harnessing the power of 'prana', which is the old Sanskrit word for breath. Breath comes from your energy or 'chi' centre, as it is called in martial arts.

The location of your chi centre, about two fingers widths below your navel, has many names. In Japan it is known as the 'hara' and in China it is the 'dantien'. The word 'chakra', derived from Sanskrit, is another way of describing an area of energy in the body. The solar plexus area is the third chakra, and is the one related to self-confidence and emotionality. (Chakras will be discussed in greater depth in Workshop 3.)

Voice coaches simply call it your 'centre'. If you are not rooted in your centre, no amount of preparation will make you more truthful or interesting. Some lucky people seem to stay 'connected up' even under pressure. They are the ones who end up in movies without any training. That is not to say that their work won't improve with further training. But it gives them a head start.

Acting coaches have always known this connection. My first mime teacher at drama school used to say, 'You can't pick up a glass with your hand. You have to pick it up from your centre.' And she would point at my solar plexus. She was right, of course, because if you pick up a glass expecting it to be full and it is empty, it will fly up into the air. We adjust to picking up different weights by preparing our stomach muscles.

I heard a story of how Marilyn Monroe's coach, Natasha Lytess, apparently annoyed Marilyn's co-star, Laurence Olivier, by frequently stepping onto the set and madly gesticulating at her own abdomen. I giggle when I catch myself standing quietly in the shadows in the corner of the studio doing exactly the same thing, albeit less overtly, by catching my actor's eye and tapping myself gently on my midriff.

Standing straight is essential to finding your chi. If you are craning forward, you won't breathe and therefore can't think. And you can't feel either. Your body has to be linked to your needs – you can't be angry on one foot, suave if you crumple, impress with your chin jutting forwards.

Watch any leading film actor. See how straight they stand or how they lean back rather than forwards when they are relaxed. When the cat walks past the camera, we can't take our eyes off it. It is comfortable in its own skin so we are impelled to watch. You need to be comfortable in yours. **3.2**

Straight and Strong

Let me prove my point. Posture is deeply linked to breathing and relaxation. Because the larynx is suspended by muscles and ligaments and is not directly connected to another jointed part of the body, it is greatly affected by posture.

> Sit upright with your eyes closed, breathing through your nose. As you feel the breath entering and leaving the body, collapse a little at the chest and feel the restriction. Return to an upright posture. Now lift your shoulders a little and feel how that affects your breathing. Stick your chin forward and you will find that this position has nearly cut off the breath altogether.

And yet so many actors at a casting call lean forwards, resting their elbows on their knees and read from there. The breathing is cut off, and therefore the emotional channel is cut off as the chin is thrust forward. But of course, the actor feels protected!

Yes, there are times that you would genuinely lean forward in your role but you wouldn't need to sustain that position for long. There are roles that feel sorry for themselves and crumple and this may be the right way to play them, but be aware that they are not appealing to us. Remember, we are more attracted to people who are strong and brave. Also, you will not look so good in the camera if you crane towards it. Your chin will look bigger and we won't get the full impact of your eyes. So, it is worth finding other choices when you can. And be sure it is the role that needs to lean forward. The main drive that takes your body forward is your own actor's insecurity.

Since, quite understandably, you want to do well, it is hard to resist the impulse to push towards the other person or to come 'off-centre' in a desire to please. But we are more drawn to you if you are comfortable in your own skin and relaxed back.

Instant Posture

 Take your shoes off and stand up with your weight on both feet. Rock slowly backwards and forwards until you find your centre of balance. Don't be too far back on your heels, or too far onto your toes.

 Play around with where the weight is on your feet until you feel grounded.

Now take your weight forward a little so that your big toes feel the floor. (It is only your weight that should move a little forward, your head is still lengthening out of your back and your chin is not jutting out.)

In this position with the weight slightly forwards, greet some imaginary people. Now take the weight centrally onto your feet and greet them again. Could you feel that you were more engaged the first time and that your voice probably sounded brighter, more welcoming? With your feet grounded evenly, you sounded strong and firm and maybe felt more in control, but not as warm.

Now put one foot slightly behind you and take your weight back onto it and greet them again. Your voice will have dropped in energy. You may 'see' yourself doing the action. This position is for reflection. It takes you inwards so that you deal with your thoughts. Our body and minds are inextricably linked.

All these positions are good and right at different times but you need to be in the one that serves your intention.

Now feel the floor firmly with your feet, with your weight evenly balanced. (You can still be aware of your big toe making slight contact with the floor.)

Unlock your knees, feel your back lengthening. Circle your arms backwards, then let them drop, taking your shoulders with them. Lift your shoulders and let them drop.

Drop your head, let your mouth open a little and circle your head gently from one shoulder to the other. (Don't take your head round to the back.)

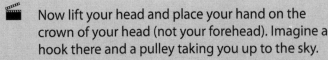

- Now lift your head and place your hand on the crown of your head (not your forehead). Imagine a hook there and a pulley taking you up to the sky.

- Drop your hand by your side and go up onto your toes, continuing to imagine that hook lifting you skywards.

- Now lower your feet and really make contact with the floor whilst still imagining your head going upwards.

- Your chin should be parallel to the floor, not tilted up or pushed down. ⊙ **3.2.b**

In future workshops, we'll call this position being 'at ease'. *Sit or stand up straight, Think, And Remember to breathe.* Like so many simple things, it is easy to know but harder for the body to remember to do it. More games and exercises will be found in Workshop 3.

In the meantime – don't lean forward, don't lean forward, *don't lean forward!*

The Power of Preparation
How to Rehearse Alone

When you start to rehearse, whether you only have a day before the casting, or a month before filming starts for a big role, I would always suggest that your first rehearsals are done with no regard to performance itself. You need to find your 'real life' first. By that, I mean you should rehearse with no thought for the camera angles or continuity requirements or constrictions of space.

Surround yourself with the trappings of the world you are to inhabit. Use as many props as you need, as much space as you would have and move where you will. People your world with real or imagined parents, sisters, lovers, bosses, friends. Do you have pets, livestock, stuffed animals? You have to establish your imaginative reality before you can start worrying about technical problems or honing down the props and moves to make the continuity less of a burden. In terms of the camera – unless you are directing yourself – you won't know what camera positions and angles the director has in mind anyway.

The Need – Raising the Stakes

You have to make your need strong enough to drive the action. So often, actors don't help themselves here. Your secret world is your affair so you can plant into it anything that makes what you do crucial and increases the jeopardy. There is no point in saying, 'My need is to explain to him.' My question would be, 'Why do you need to explain to him?' If you reply, 'Because I need him to know I've been unfaithful,' I would ask again, 'Why do you need him to know you've been unfaithful?' If you now said, 'Because I need him to want me again' or 'I need him to rescue me' then you would found something strong enough to play the scene.

On a scale of one to ten, your drive has to be off the scale. How much of that need you show to anyone else depends on the context. Your need may be secret or overt – that depends on the situation. 🎧 **3.9**

You can also increase the stakes and provide yourself with ammunition by giving yourself a backstory to serve you. Here are some examples from scenes I've worked on:

You are playing a scene, set in the sixties, where you have offered to marry someone to save them from being sent to the front line to fight. Why are you doing this? What if you had a boyfriend/brother/classmate who had been killed there? Of course, you do also secretly care for the person you are saving.

You are trying to make up a quarrel with your wife who won't talk to you. You come in from the garden and say, 'The blossom's out.' Why do you say that to her? Could you have planted that tree together on your first anniversary? Her refusal then to share that moment will hurt more.

You are telling your best friend that you have received a proposal of marriage that you will probably accept but you say, 'Don't be angry, I know we promised never to marry anyone.' When you prepare for this, do an improvisation (alone or together) from the past where you opened a bottle of wine and drank a toast to feminism, brotherhood or a single life. Now you have a stronger need to get your friend's approval.

You have finally got the girl who works in the library to have a coffee with you. How much do you like her? 'She's alright' was one actor's reply to this. On the contrary! You have dreamt about her for the last six months, watched her secretly every time she stacked the shelves, rehearsed how to ask her out every day. Finally you've had the courage to ask and she's accepted. Do you tell her all this or show her how much you want her? No, you play it absolutely cool, as far as your pounding heart lets you.

I once worked with a young actor playing a scene where his role was desperate to sleep with a girl he had befriended and they had arrived outside his house. He only had the line, 'Come inside'. 'What do you want?' I asked. 'I want her to come into the house,' he replied. 'Why do you want her to come into the house?' I pursued. 'To make her a cup of tea,' he said.

My comment on that is, if this is a film about a man who wants to make a woman a cup of tea, I don't think I'll bother seeing it! Films are about pursuing what you want in spite of obstacles. The conflict that arises provides the drama. In trying to get what we want, we try many routes. When we come up against an obstacle – either within ourselves or from outside – we deflect and try again. So we are reacting against whatever comes up to stop us. You need to explore what causes your reaction.

Maybe your role says very little. That doesn't mean there aren't any needs. What is it you want but can never ask for? What keeps you rooted to the spot? What obstacle stops you from leaving? Or what titillates you so much you want to stay? What are you watching, listening to, thinking about? How does your environment impinge on you? Some wonderful directors like Jonathan Miller or Robert Altman give whole life stories to the tiniest roles in their productions.

Beware of the 'How to' Demons

Who am I? You need to know the differences between yourself and you in the role. You need to work only on the differences, the rest you have already.

Where am I? You need to know everything about your circumstances, the times and place you live in and everything about the life you lead.

What are my relationships? You need to know the relationship (as you see it) to everyone else in your life.

What do I want? What do you need? What drives you? You need to know clearly what you want. And that need has to be gnawing away at you, guiding everything you do. Though not necessarily shown to those around you.

What stops me? What is the obstacle you have to overcome? It might be inside you or involve other people or circumstances.

How do I get what I want? The physical and psychological actions that we do to fulfil our needs, and deal with whatever gets in our way, are what occupy our waking lives. In my first book, *Acting for Film: Truth 24 Times a Second*, I suggested that you write down your actions for each 'beat', such as 'I cajole...', 'I plead...', and so on. I did end that book by saying, 'This is what I believe at this moment – don't hold me to it, I may change my mind.'

Well, I have changed my mind in this instance. I have become increasingly suspicious of mapping out 'actions' or 'intentions'. I think that it might work in theatre, when you are rehearsing with other people and making joint decisions. But I don't see how you can do it for film when you have no idea what obstacles the other actors will throw in your path. You can't decide your reactions when you don't know what you are reacting to. And mapping out a course of beats and actions can get dangerously close to mapping out how you are going to play it. And that is something you can never do. Every moment has to be fresh and immediate.

Of course, in order to pursue that all-consuming need or drive, you will be *taking* actions at every second. You *will* 'plead', 'cajole', and take a million other ways to get what you want. But these actions need to happen spontaneously in reaction to the obstacles that the other roles or the situation throw up. Of course you must take action to get what you want. Of course you must have intentions and actions, and you can explore different ones in rehearsal. But these cannot be planned and set in advance when you may not know even who you are playing the scene with, let alone what 'actions' he or she will be playing. And you can't be thinking about these decisions as you play and still be alive in the moment.

Beware of planning. Beware of those 'how to' demons – 'How should I say this?', 'How will I react?' The most common advice I give to actors on set is 'Don't know what you are going to say next. Don't know what will happen next.' You will take action because you are trying to get what you want, moment to moment. And you will keep meeting obstacles that will shift and change the way you react throughout the scene, but you cannot prepare these reactions. They have to happen in the immediacy of dealing with whatever comes up as you pursue what you want. They have to be organic and you must learn to trust your impulses.

Once you have done your homework and worked out what you need and where that need changes, you have simply to try to get it. Just as you would in life.

Dare to let go and be brave enough not to plan. I worked with a lovely actor in a workshop in Cologne, Germany. She had come from theatre and tended to plot everything out and to make decisions. She found just letting things happen very frightening as she felt her work went out of her control. After our five days of intensive work together, she had found a new freedom, and some time afterwards she wrote to me about her next experience working. Here is what she wrote:

“ Last week I worked on a TV series and I played a
traumatised woman who hadn't left the house for
five years. In the end her sister is found to be the
murderer and we had to play a very emotional scene
together. And you know what? I managed something
I'd never managed before. I cried without any help. I
repeated it three times. I could never have done that
without the week we spent together. And you know
why? Because I kept thinking before each take: 'I
don't know what will happen now. I don't know if I
will cry or not, we'll see.' And so it happened again
and again. And I said to myself, 'You don't need to
feel safe. You are not in a safe situation.'

So I echo her: you don't need to feel safe. You are not in a
safe situation. And with that bravery will come a great
release. You are not responsible for the outcome. You are not
responsible for the film. You are not responsible for making
the audience understand. Unlike theatre, it is not your job
carry the narrative – the filmmaker will do that. You are only
responsible for committing to the moment, believing it completely and pursuing what you want and need. Dare not to
know what will happen next.

It has to be like life. When you enter the situation, you have
an idea of who you are, where you are, what your relationship is to the other person, and what you want. But how you
will (or won't) get it is entirely dependent on what happens
moment to moment.

Which, by the way, is also why you can't demand anything
from another actor. In life you get what you get. Nothing is
gained by asking another actor to play the scene in a way that
suits you and it is not your place to do so. Only the director
can ask an actor for a particular performance. Because, ultimately, she or he is the omnipotent puppet-master!

I was once the acting coach to a young woman on a movie
and there was another coach working with the leading lady.

The night before the scene, this other coach came up to me and said that her actor had asked whether I would get my actor to play the scene in a particular way to help her own performance. I listened politely to my instructions, nodded and told her it would be fine. I then, of course, did nothing of the sort. And it was fine.

Of course, on the technical side, any major moves or gestures that evolved from your position of 'not knowing' will now be filmed – and set in stone – in the master shot and will have to be found in subsequent set-ups. But that only applies to the physical moves themselves, not the inner drives and thoughts, which will be subtly different each time you do it. You will have to make sure that real impulses take you to the same moves again and again. But that's for your 'stage-manager head' to deal with – your innocent acting self must not know they are going to happen. And we'll cope with the technical when we come to the filming itself.

Get Out of Your Own Way

❝ Sometimes there is a special happiness in being a film director. An unrehearsed expression is born, just like that, and the camera registers that expression… it is possible I live for those brief moments. Like a pearl fisher.

Ingmar Bergman
The Magic Lantern

Of course we use our heads for conscious thought and so will your 'role', but don't interfere with the organic life of your role by standing outside and thinking as an observer. You must allow the unrehearsed to happen. That is what I mean by 'get out of your own way'.

There is an inbuilt censor inside most of us. This little devil will pop up with comments like, 'That looked silly', 'That sounded wrong', 'You weren't really feeling that'. Or your internal director comes in, 'You should move now', 'Do something with your hand'. Ignore these comments – don't let your head get in your way!

Are you on that back foot when it is your intention to engage with someone else rather than to reflect upon something? If you are trying to welcome, find out, listen, watch or take action – then you won't have your weight back. If you are looking at a piece of art and deciding how it affects you, weighing up the pros and cons, or standing back emotionally from the situation – then you may have. But if it is you, the actor, on the back foot because you are defensive, shy or nervous – then this is a sure way to let that devilish little censor invade your thoughts and flash up a picture of yourself looking awkward.

Jump without a safety net. Let go of your control. Be brave, brave, brave. Really listen. Really look.

Put your attention on your fellow actors, your situation and the world around you. How do your words affect the other person? You might be walking a tightrope in this situation with everything you say, choosing the words as you go and constantly checking that you are saying the right things. You might be in love with them, watching whether it is reciprocated. Sensing their warmth with every skin cell, even if you're not looking at them. Maybe you are with your boss, not knowing if you are going to be promoted or fired, trying to look calm and confident with your heart beating painfully, listening to every nuance of his speech patterns. Trying to find out where you stand. Allow yourself to take the time to receive from the other person. You are not doing a scene – you are living a life.

Whilst you are talking to them, how much do you need to look at the other character? Are you scrutinising them overtly or snatching quick glances whilst playing it cool or engaged in another activity?

We usually have more than one thing taking our attention at the same time. What else are you doing in this world whilst you engage in this conversation? We are often involved in a secondary activity as we deal with the main business in hand. We might be noticing the tree outside the window, chopping an onion or folding a sheet. And whilst we need to win the argument, or find out if they have a lover, or show our child we love them and want to look at the picture they've drawn, we also need to get the supper on or the bed made.

I think we can only have one conscious thought at a time, but we can flip between thoughts in a split second. If you are talking to your child and the pot boils over, you leap into action with your whole attention on turning off the heat before you return to your child. Whilst you think one thing, though, your hands can continue to work merrily with their motor memory; your eyes and ears still take in what is around you and feed it into your subconscious. This is part of your survival mechanism. If something suddenly impinges upon you, like the pot overflowing, it will leap into your conscious and you will take action to deal with it.

Building a Life

In Workshop 3, there will be techniques to add to your tool-box – different routes into your role. But however you do it, you need a sense of the continuum – that these moments we are filming are just part of the real ongoing life you, as the role, are leading. 🎧 **2.9**

For example, if you have one scene where you are breaking off your relationship, then you need to have been in love before you can fall out of love. Because you are working in film or television, you might not meet your lover until you get to set, but there is still work you can do on your own.

You can improvise alone. You could get up in the morning and dress to meet them for your first date. You can be waiting in the restaurant with the engagement ring in your pocket. Writing invitations for the wedding. You can be planning how to decorate the nursery for your first child. When you cook the meal – it's their favourite food. When the telephone rings – it could be them. Then you have a past to turn your back on. Then your anger will be stronger, your tears more bitter because you have loved them.

Don't just think these things, act them out. By engaging all your senses, the whole of you will be involved in the creation of this life, not just your brain. Your imaginary world will become real, concrete. And your body will retain its own memories. 🎧 **3.3, 3.4, 3.5**

If you don't know who is to play the role of your lover, you can use someone from your own life or from your imagination for your preparation. Curiously, when you meet the real person, your imaginary lover will magically morph into the skin of the actor in front of you. Whereas, if you don't do any work beforehand, you won't have enough time with the actor to create a real relationship. Some people use substitution to superimpose the person they have been imagining over the actor. I don't believe you need to do that. You can instinctively endow the actual actor with the attributes of your imaginary lover and then allow the reality of your new partner to take over. As you look at them you will find specific things that you used to love in them, but now you hate.

If your partner in the scene will work with you when you meet, so much the better. Before you do your breaking-up scene, if nothing else, hold each other close before you film. Then pull apart and don't look at them again until you play the scene. 💿 **3.4**

You can also 'bind' with objects that are important to you during your preparation work. Shut your eyes and hold a prop tightly that is important to you to make it part of your life. If you are leaving the house you love, press your hands against a wall, or the tree in the garden – let it take your weight. Now pull away roughly. You will feel a sense of loss. If you are leaving your native land – do the same with the soil – let it take your weight, then abruptly leave it for ever. 💿 **3.4**

Pictures and Memories

Remember that when we tell someone something that has happened to us, we have clear, specific pictures in our heads. In telling the story, we move between these pictures and our desire to share them with the listener. In the course of this, we pull up words, censor them and find others. We gesticulate, sometimes to convey the picture we are seeing, sometimes with the sense-memory of what happened in our bodies, sometimes metaphorically or geographically. We tend to laugh at the worst moments of the story. 💿 **1.1, 2.1, 2.7**

The best way to observe this closely is to watch other people – in the pub or on the train or at a dinner party. The next best way is to watch documentaries. For example, *The World at War*, the documentary series made by Thames Television in the 1970s, was able to find people who still had clear memories of living through the Second World War. The series is filled with people telling terrible events that they relive and tell with the kind of energy that is rarely seen in the work of actors. The words are said factually, and if emotion wells up, it is dealt with and put aside to stop it getting in the way of the importance of telling the story. As the speaker gets more and more involved in reliving the event, they become more and more physically involved, as if it is happening at this moment. If the story starts with something mundane, or even happy, and moves towards an awful conclusion, each moment is told through what was felt at the time. The end does not shadow the start of the narrative. The speaker reaches it, as it were, in real time. At the worst moment, they will often smile or even laugh. 💿 **2.7**

The documentary film *Man on Wire* (2008) also contains fine examples of people being interviewed thirty or so years on and seeing the events happen again, in their memories, with the same clarity and emotional surge that they felt the first time round.

So often the actor is trying to 'see' a story for the first time, then the energy goes inwards and the voice becomes coloured by the emotion that the actor feels about the situation when viewing it from the outside. When someone tells a real story, they have actually *experienced* it. It has already happened and now they are 'seeing' it again and sharing those pictures. The only way to make a text come alive is to act it out physically first. Then the energy will go in the right direction. 💿 **2.8**

Unconscious versus Conscious

Sometimes actors ask me, 'What is the point of all the homework and preparation if, in the here and now of "doing", you tell me I have to forget it all and just react in the moment?'

My only answer is that it has to be like life. Over the years, you have built an iceberg of experiences and beliefs. The top of the iceberg is seen by the world and you are consciously aware of how it drives you in your day-to-day existence. But seven-eighths of your iceberg lies submerged beneath your normal consciousness, yet influences how you deal with people and situations and your attitudes to everything. In the meantime, you go about life pursuing what you want and need through conscious thought, decision and action, without thinking about this submerged history.

If you try to create a 'character' in a few short days or weeks from an empty vessel, it cannot begin to have the depth that you have built up over the course of twenty, thirty or seventy years of life. Freud saw the unconscious mind as a store of collected information, memories, desires and needs that we are not even aware of ourselves. Jonathan Miller directed me many years ago and instilled in me a respect for these tiny, seeming negligible details of life that build to create lives of considerable depth. He talks about a pre-Freudian view of the unconscious as 'enabling'. This 'enabling unconscious' allows you to respond and act spontaneously out of your stored knowledge that you are unaware of on a conscious level.

Your own underlying store of acquired knowledge and refer-ences is what makes you a unique human being. It means that 'you' in this role will already be different to any other actor's interpretation. But you can add to this store and change your attitudes by your work on the specific life of the role and allow this new awareness to sink down into your subcon-scious. And, inevitably, the act of playing this role will add to your own unconscious store, which is how you grow as an actor.

To go about storing this new knowledge, you have to know, in concrete and specific terms, everything about the life your role has led. This means going on asking yourself, time and time again, why your role reacts like that, what specific incident has led you to behave in that particular way? How often does Harry come to dinner, when did the relationship begin? Who asked who out first? Why does he turn down your sauce? What happened last time you served it? Why haven't you seen your mother since last year? What does she mean by asking you what you did last weekend? Was it her birthday? And so on and so on. It is like picking your way through a tangled ball of string, unravelling as you go until you can travel its length.

This analysis of your role, the physical preparation, the improvisations and all the other work you put into your rehearsal turn the prism of your own possibilities to reflect new mental and physical knowledge. To pursue my metaphor, it is as if your unconscious submerged iceberg is shifting, melting and re-forming as you add to it and adjust it through your work on your part. Then, like life, you forget it and simply deal with the conscious needs and thoughts of your role, trusting that this new unconscious will bleed into the work, feed the conscious and emerge when necessary.

If, at any time, you try to show us this underlying work, you will cease to be truthful. You should let go of any desire to reflect this homework, and simply act and react in the moment.

For example, you are playing a woman whose husband has recently died. You are cooking a meal for your son who is due home any minute. You think about his arrival, you smile as you stir carrots into the stew, hoping he will eat them without noticing. Your attention is on the simmering pan and the texture of the stew. As you stir the pan, your attention is taken by a spider on the wall. You feel an immediate surge of panic and nausea clutches your abdomen. For a moment you freeze with fear and then you find the strength to grab a mop and flick it out of the window. You feel a sense of exhilaration, then think of your husband and tears run down your cheeks as you realise that you can never again call on him to deal with spiders. You look out of the window at the tree that you planted together last year and say out loud, 'You would have been proud of me.' You smile, brush away the tears, look at the clock and realise your son is due any minute. You continue with the stew, absorbed in its preparation, humming a tune.

The work on this scenario might include:

- What do your husband and son look like? What are those relationships like? Do some improvisations about each of them.

- Where is your son? Does he like your stew? Why doesn't he like carrots? How hard have you tried to get him to eat them? Why does the stew need to be ready on time? Have you made it before or is it a new recipe?

- Why are you so afraid of spiders? Do an improvisation of a particular event that precipitated this phobia. Is it important that the spider doesn't stop you cooking? Is that what makes you find the bravery to deal with the spider?

- How did you meet your husband? What did he do for a living? When did he die? How did he die? How have you coped since? When did your husband first rescue you from a spider? Was it on your first date? What is this tree that you have planted? What did it mean to you both? Is this the first time you have dealt with a spider since he died? Did he use the same mop to rid you of them?

- What is the tune you are humming at the end? What does it mean to you?

And so on and so on. Each decision is yours to make, and the more compelling you make your needs and the more jeopardy you evoke from the obstacles, the richer you make the scene. As you look around the room you are sitting in as you read this, you will have some story, memory or feeling about everything you look at. Your relationships and life are as complex and extraordinary as anything you conjure out of fiction. So don't be bland in your decisions, let your imagination serve you.

 Make everything about your world specific. Keep asking yourself questions and act out the answers.

 Make it *your* world. Remember to say 'I' when speaking as your role – not 'he' or 'she'. Why put any layer between yourself and the role you have to play? **1.4**

But having done all this work, remember most of that iceberg lies beneath the surface and only deal with each moment as it comes up. Give your conscious attention to the stew, the time constraint, and coping with the spider. If you have done your homework well and fed it into your subconscious, your emotion will rise up of its own accord as the memory of your dead husband flashes into your mind as you see the tree. What you can't do is to play the scene as a woman in mourning for her husband. You cannot try to feel sad.

People assume that if you are carrying the weight of pain and grief that it will permeate everything you do. But if you have had a terrible past and are out shopping or the doorbell rings, you cope with the task in hand in an everyday way, not as a person with a terrible past. Unless you are still in shock and trauma or want sympathy, the grocer or the postman will not know what lies behind your normal manner.

You Gotta Have Attitude

You in the role have to have attitude. By that, I don't necessarily mean 'attitude' like Angelina Jolie in *Girl, Interrupted* (1999) or Marlon Brando in *On the Waterfront* (1954) or James Dean in *East of Eden* (1955) – though that can be gripping – I mean that you must have a view on the world.

This view of the world involves how you fit into it and how you relate to others. Everyone must view the world differently or else we would all think, vote and shop the same way. Everyone is propelled into action by their own different angle on life. Everyone acts in an inevitable way given their perspective on life at that given moment.

This world view also involves how you perceive your status and that of others. You may be playing a high-status role like Cate Blanchett in *Elizabeth* (1998), or someone who thinks he is high status like Arthur Lowe in *Dad's Army* (TV), or a domineering down-and-out like Donald Pleasence in *The Caretaker* (1963), or you may be a put-upon sales executive like Jack Lemmon in *Glengarry Glen Ross* (1992). This attitude may change during the course of the story and will be affected by those you interact with. Sometimes the changes will be overt and recognised by the other characters, like the rise of *The Admirable Crichton* (1957), where a servant becomes the master after a shipwreck, or Boudu in Jean Renoir's 1932 classic *Boudu Sauvé des Eaux* (remade as *Down and Out in Beverly Hills* in 1986), where a tramp becomes richer than his benefactors. Or the shifts of status may be subtle like the power games played by James Fox and Dirk Bogarde in Pinter's *The Servant* (1963) or the class attitudes within *Gosford Park* (2001). They may be overtly sexual like *Last Tango in Paris* (1972) or deadly yet delicate as in *Dangerous Liaisons* (1988) and *Ridicule* (1996). Or just deadly like *Wars of the Roses* (1989).

Although the internet changes all the time, with the exception of *The Admirable Crichton* (1957), clips from all the productions mentioned above can currently be viewed on YouTube. Particularly worth watching for status interaction are the clips from *Glengarry Glen Ross* (1992) between Jack Lemmon as real estate salesman Shelley Levene and the bullying Blake, played superbly by Alec Baldwin. The whole film is an example of great ensemble playing.

Like all great performances, Kate Winslet's role in *Revolutionary Road* (2008), Peter O'Toole in *Lawrence of Arabia* (1962) or as Fisk Senior in *Dean Spanley* (2008), Johnny Depp's Captain Jack Sparrow in the *Pirates of the Caribbean* movies (2003–), Jeremy Irons as Claus von Bülow in *Reversal of Fortune* (1990) or James Corden's Smithy in *Gavin and Stacey* (TV) are unique creations with distinct attitudes. These attitudes stem from their roles' values and beliefs and how these collide with the world around them and the values and beliefs of that society. It depends upon how the roles see their status themselves and how others see them. They are complex human beings. It is hard to think of any memorable performance that does not carry a specific and distinctive attitude to life.

Yet I observe many actors only learning their lines and worrying about how to say them. There should be no question of a right or a wrong way to say a line, as long as you make complete and specific sense of it. It should arise, unbidden, out of a desire to fulfil whatever need you in the role have in that moment of time. And that desire has arisen out of your choices about your role's distinct view of the world, attitude to it, status within it and the situation.

The important thing is that you can never be neutral. You have an opinion about everything and everyone. Or you have an attitude to the fact that you don't or won't. That is what makes you a real living human being.

Being in the Right Subtext

We've talked about emotion and how, if you've done your preparation, it will well up without you having to dig inside to try to bring it up. But when it does erupt out of you, how much do you want the other character to know?

Pursuing my geophysical metaphors, you could have a volcano under your icy calm (there is one in Iceland!). It lies unseen beneath your iceberg, emotion puffing out in little gasps of steam whilst you try to keep a cool surface. Or you could give in, release the maelstrom and be engulfed completely by a whirlpool of misery!

A more sensible way of looking at this is to ask how much is going on in subtext and how much is overt? And this doesn't only relate to emotion. How much do you want the other person to know about anything and how much do you in the role know? If what you say is what you mean, if what you feel is what's on show – there's no subtext. If there are subtle nuances you are not showing, if you are not telling the whole truth, if you are not letting other people in the scene see everything you feel – that's subtext. If you are lying completely, if you are playing a game, if you are in disguise – that's subtext.

The eighteenth-century French politician, Talleyrand, claimed that language was given to us to conceal our thoughts. In the world of *Dangerous Liaisons*, it was safer to deal in subtext!

The important thing is, which subtext? Here are at least three kinds of subtext:

1. You want the other person to guess your subtext.
2. You do not want them to guess your subtext at any cost.
3. You (in the role) do not realise you are using subtext.

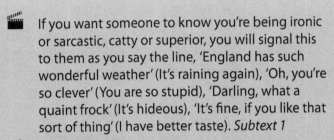

If you want someone to know you're being ironic or sarcastic, catty or superior, you will signal this to them as you say the line, 'England has such wonderful weather' (It's raining again), 'Oh, you're so clever' (You are so stupid), 'Darling, what a quaint frock' (It's hideous), 'It's fine, if you like that sort of thing' (I have better taste). *Subtext 1*

If you are lying or trying not to offend, bluffing that you know something or fighting for your life, you will not want the other person to read what lies behind the lines: 'I was with the guys at the pub' (I was with my mistress), 'You still look as beautiful as you ever did' (I love you even though we're getting old), 'The Minister has all the figures to hand' (The Minister doesn't have a clue), 'I have never seen him before in my life' (I shot him). *Subtext 2*

We use subtext a lot in an unconscious manner. We want to elicit a response from others to our lifestyle, our wealth or our class. When you do your preparation for the role, you have to dig out these deep drives but when in the role, you will be unaware of them: 'I can't cook a thing' (I want you to know I'm much too interesting to do housework), 'I can't even afford a bike' (I want you to feel sorry for me), 'I can't bear the word "lounge"' (I want you to know I'm posh.) *Subtext 3*

The third type of subtext can be a permanent way of responding. Our early conditioning can remain long after our lifestyle changes. I have a friend who was a penniless writer until he was forty; now he is comfortably well off, but any reference to buying something expensive will bring immediate, and endearing, incredulity ('I want you to know I haven't money to waste like that!'). I've moved to the countryside but am very quick to point out to my neighbours how I travel to London each week ('I want you to know I'm still very sophisticated – not a country hick!'). We often hang on to our notions of where we are in the social pecking order, how we feel about politics and what we should wear long after our situation has changed, the reasons for our decisions have altered and the world about us has moved on. It is what makes us who we are. And it is buried in this unconscious subtext.

So which subtext are you using? Another way of avoiding the danger described in Workshop 1 of 'showing' an audience is to decide what subtext you are in. If you should be in Subtext 2 – making sure that the other character doesn't guess what lies beneath the words you say – you must be careful not to slip into Subtext 1. If you do that, you will be 'signalling' and it will be signalling to us, the viewers, in case we didn't get the point!

You have to remember to be as convincing as you would be in life. We are very good at lying. We do it all the time. We may justify it as not hurting other people's feelings, but we do it all the same. Every time you say that you'd love to come to dinner when you'd rather stay at home – you are lying convincingly. Every time you tell your guest that the broken glass/plate/vase (that was a family heirloom) doesn't matter a jot – you are lying convincingly. Every time I tell my publisher that I won't be late for the deadline – I am lying. And sometimes, even I may believe the lie.

A good director will find a way to tell the story. If it is important to the plot that the subtext is revealed, then there will be a close-up that catches you in a private moment at the sink or looking out the window or staring at your whisky when you are left alone, when your mask will drop and we will see what you are thinking. Just like life – when you groan as you walk away from the dinner invitation or moan to your family as you sweep up the shards of glass after the guests have gone.

If Kevin Spacey had shown us the subtext in *The Usual Suspects* (1995) there would have been no film. If Philip Seymour Hoffman had let us know what happened with the young choirboy, there would be no doubt in *Doubt* (2008). If the past had been revealed to us in *Caché* (2005), nothing would be hidden.

 Check out on DVD – or YouTube – Kevin Spacey in *The Usual Suspects*, giving nothing away, as Keyser Soze beneath the persona of 'Verbal'.

All the work leads to the same thing: are you committed absolutely to your imaginary world? Once you have done your preparation, built your life and know your specific need, are you involved only in your conscious action to get what you want? Are you in the right chakra (see Workshop 3)? Are you using the right subtext?

Uncovering the Truth

All human beings use subtext some of the time. Even the most truthful people cannot tell all the truth all the time. And not all subtext is about lying. It can be about the thoughts that rise up but are too complicated or too painful or too personal to be told.

A script will often have lines that end with a dash or an ellipsis (i.e. a dot, dot, dot…). This may be an interruption from the other character but it is often an indication that you are censoring these thoughts that rise unbidden. It is vitally important that you know how you would have completed that sentence if you had not censored yourself. You also need to know why you are not able to say these things. What pictures and memories rise up, what glance to the other person told you this was a dangerous thing to reveal, what would these words expose about your innermost thoughts?

Here is a short excerpt from Ingmar Bergman's film, *Face to Face* (1976). Jenny is a psychiatrist who has tried to commit suicide. Eric is her husband who has flown back urgently from a conference in Chicago to visit her in hospital. He has just told her he will have to return there the next day:

JENNY
Poor you!

ERIK
Oh, I'm all right.

JENNY
The trouble I cause.

ERIK
It would have been awful if you... I'd
never have... In all my life I've never
been so...

JENNY
Forgive me!

ERIK
Why did you do it?

JENNY
Forgive me. Forgive me.

Here, the actor playing Erik has to know precisely what he was going to say, but couldn't. He might have been going to say, 'It would have been awful if you had killed yourself. I'd never have forgiven myself. In all my life I've never been so scared.' That would be my guess.

But he might have been going to say, 'It would have been awful if you'd ended up as a vegetable. I'd never have forgiven you. In all my life I've never been so angry.' Only you can decide what those 'dot dot dots' are from your work on the role.

Jenny may guess what he is going to say and wants to save him from showing her his vulnerability or stop him making her feel guilty – so the last 'dot dot dots' of Erik's may be an interruption by Jenny.

What you can't do is be generalised or just see the line tailing away into insignificance. Something powerful in the picture you have conjured up, or how it makes you feel, or what you suddenly see in the other person's face has made you stop or made you interrupt. The truth is too hard, discomforting or dangerous to speak.

Always say your 'dot dot dot' lines in full first so you know what you are censoring. An excellent device to find out what subtext lies under your lines and, indeed, to find out if you are in subtext at all, is to speak your thoughts aloud and then say your lines. This will show you when you are revealing the whole truth and when you are covering it up. And what you are covering up. 💿 **2.9**

Here is a short scene from Harold Pinter's treatment of Joseph Conrad's novel *Victory*. He wrote it for the director Richard Lester, but sadly the finance was never found. It is a superb script. If you want to work on subtext, I highly recommend Pinter's screenplays.

It is set in 1900. Lena is an English girl who left her father in a home for incurables after he had a stroke (her mother had run away), and she joined a travelling orchestra to play violin. She is working in a hotel in Surabaya, Java, when Heyst finds her. Heyst lives alone on a tiny uninhabited island where he had a mining business that failed. He has travelled to Surabaya to visit his doctor and get provisions. He sees Lena being mistreated by the hotelier and the manager of the orchestra and, because he is both attracted to her and sorry for her, takes her off at dawn in his boat to his island. This is the following day. He has given her his room. He wants to make love to her.

```
EXT. FOREST.

Heyst and Lena walking under enormous
trees festooned with creepers. Great
splashes of light.

They emerge onto the highest point on
the island. Rocks.

She looks out to sea.

The sea and horizon. heat haze.

EXT. LENA AND HEYST.

She shuts her eyes.

                    LENA
        It makes my head swim.

                    HEYST
                 Too big?

                    LENA
        Too lonely. All that water. All that
                    light.

                    HEYST
            Come into the shade.

They sit under a tree.
```

This is a great scene to speak the thoughts aloud and then to say the lines. Don't go into a stream of consciousness but simply find the one thought you have that you don't want the other person to know. For example, *What have I done? Can I trust him?* = 'It makes my head swim.' *She's frightened, I must reassure her.* = 'Too big?'

The scene isn't about being dizzy or finding the shade, although, on a surface level, those things are true – the sea is vast and the sun is hot. Heyst doesn't want Lena to know that he desires her that much (later, he rapes her and then apologises for it. He has been alone a long time, and she is beautiful). Lena doesn't want Heyst to know how confused she is or that she wants him to love her. Or any of the other possibilities that you might decide.

One watch point with this: it is all too easy to be vague or superficial with your subtext. A line such as 'You're always so lucky in love' can't just devolve into 'All right for some', 'Get you', or 'Silly cow'. You have to dig deep to find 'I hate you for being happy'. 'Do you want to come to dinner?' might not mean 'I want to be friendly', but 'I want to tell you my secret' or 'I want to make love to you tonight'.

When Subtext Disappears

Actually, whenever real emotions are involved, it is very hard to say the complete and utter truth without subtext. We are able, at moments in our life, to say, 'I love you', 'I don't love you any more', 'You are dying'. But these words cost us. They require that we put aside the social mask that gets us through life comfortably and, for that instant, wholly open ourselves up to another human being. Once said, nothing can ever be the same again. Words are powerful. Words change everything. You can never take them back.

It makes me smile (with subtext) that the work of the writer, artist, director and actor are undervalued in our commercial society. In peacetime, theatre, television and film are under-funded and relegated to the world of 'entertainment'. Yet, in times of conflict and revolution, governments censor plays and films, close theatres and ban books. The artists, writers and dream-makers are the first against the wall. So somewhere deep within us, we are aware of the power of images and words that either, as in satire, reveal the subversive subtext or are without subtext and dangerous.

In television soaps, there is less ambiguity than in other dramas. The characters wear their hearts on their sleeves and are asked to reveal what they feel in order to grip the viewer through powerful emotional intensity. Because, traditionally, these soaps have been shown at a time that most people are preparing or eating food, and the plot has to travel forwards in a short time slot, they are less subtle than drama that is shown at a later time and which is given a greater length (and more budget) to tell the story. And there has to be this overtly dramatic content to provide a cliffhanger to ensure the audience tunes in to the next episode.

This makes television soaps particularly demanding for actors, especially as they are shot at such high speed and with so little time for preparation. Because, socially, we don't often show raw emotion, you will have to work extra hard to believe that it is you 'as if' in the situation and to open yourself up to telling the truth without subtext. Otherwise, you will frown and screw your face up as you 'manufacture' this emotion. You have to avoid your own personal subtexts, 'I feel so silly', 'I hate this line', 'Can I remember this line?', 'Am I feeling enough?'

To speak without subtext appears simple, yet it can be the hardest thing we do – and the most powerful.

 **Now watch Workshop 2 on the DVD.**

Workshop
3

The Physical Life

Workshop 3

Some of the work described and shown on the DVD in the first workshop is designed primarily to stop you 'acting' and to make you connect with your role so that you are working from real drives and impulses. This is also true, for example, of Meisner's repetition exercises and the use of 'endowment' techniques advocated by many coaches.

These strategies may be all you need for many television and lightweight movies, and it is certainly crucial that at a deep level you are always working from yourself. Drawing only from your own memories and personal experiences for the great roles, however, is likely to be essentially reductive. There are places that our film selves may have to go emotionally, symbolically or spiritually that most of us have never known in our own lives – and may not wish to. Great actors find a depth to their work that goes beyond the everyday and take us on a journey that pushes our understanding of human nature and the forces that govern it.

To do this, you need to explore your deepest imaginative senses and through your body you can sense things that your brain may not understand. You can tap into a greater universal truth and channel emotions that you personally may never have felt.

By working through breath, body, imagination and changing habitual patterns, you can release a deep creative power within you. This workshop takes you away from the technical requirements of the camera and allows you to explore these possibilities.

The Actor's Crucible: Physiological Alchemy

The Power of the Breath

You need the alchemy of breathing to effect any kind of transformation, give you power or breathe life into the written word. You know about abdominal-diaphragmatic breath already, but let's go further and then do some practical work. Why would you need to think so much about breathing for screen work? Film is a naturalistic medium, isn't it? You don't need to project your voice or sustain a note. You're not going to deliver a Shakespearean soliloquy or rouse a rabble from a podium or carry out a conversation whilst having a sword fight, are you? Well, you may be called upon to do any or all of these. But even if you don't need to project or speak verse, you need, like life, to breathe to stay alive in the role. And by breathing, I mean relaxed breathing – not snatching or holding your breath.

Voice is the Cinderella of the film industry. This is because, as sound and picture are recorded separately, the sound is laid on afterwards and very often the finished product doesn't contain the original recording. Months after shooting, actors go into a small voice studio and record a new dialogue track.

Breathing is fundamental to life – and cannot be applied later. Even if you redo the voice track, the acting that you did at the time was indivisibly linked to breath and voice. I have been told by actors on set that they don't want to use full voice or think about matching their voice to their actions and needs because they will 'loop' it later.

I remember one 'sword and horse' film in particular, where this excuse was used by several of the actors to avoid committing to full voice during filming. But when you view the footage, you can see that, on screen, the actor doesn't look fully engaged in the task of riding the horse or digging the grave – the energy just isn't there. And that can never be put back in a sound booth at a later date.

Because, these days, we are mostly 'social speakers' who let words bubble out pretty easily, we have to work extra-hard when we play roles from an earlier time or who are engaged in a physical life, where the voice must be firmly rooted in the body and the strength of words has to be found to deal with life and death decisions.

Presence, charisma, being centred, star quality – call it what you will – it is hard to define and yet every good actor has it. So do animals or children who are at ease in their own bodies. They are not trying to please or achieve; they are simply *being*. Even if the role is doing a task that involves high activity and jeopardy, the actor must not be working from a state of unconscious tension. You may find a tautness that arises from the conditions and situation of the scene. Don't confuse this genuine energy that you need to deal with the task in hand, with a state of held tension within yourself that can only block you as an actor.

By using abdominal-diaphragmatic breathing, finding a state of ease, taking your space and resisting the urge to push forwards, you will become centred. And you will acquire 'presence'.

Seven was a magic number in ancient philosophy. It was supposed to govern our health and the ages of man. So, here are seven vital reasons for working on your breathing technique for film!

1. Fighting Lions

Filming is extremely stressful. There you are, standing in front of a camera with a crew of three hundred people all making a noise and doing their own thing. You've had about five hours sleep because you were in make-up at six a.m. Suddenly the First Assistant Director shouts, 'Quiet everyone. Going for a take.' You hear the different departments confirming, 'Camera speed', 'Sound speed', then 'Action!' and the whole studio is so quiet you can hear your heart beating. And they all wait, looking at you. I defy anyone to stay cool – not to feel the heart racing, the senses quicken. ⊙ **3.0**

Now a gasp is a very useful kind of breathing if you need to attack the lion that has just run into the studio. As adrenalin pumps around the body, this sharp intake of breath rushes oxygen into the brain and gives a vital moment when all the senses work on overdrive and you can hit the lion with your prop sword or flee for your life through the exit doors.

The problem is that you are 'fighting lions' for hours at a time on set and the usefulness of this kind of breathing is very short-lived. After a few moments, because only the top part of your lungs is getting enough oxygen and there is an imbalance between the oxygen coming in and the carbon dioxide going out, you start to suffer physical changes. Your hands start to shake, your knees feel weak, your head feels dizzy, your voice is breathy, and you've forgotten your lines. Stage fright is just as common on the screen! I have watched from behind the monitor as many actors dried take after take on the one sentence they had to say.

Obviously, if the situation demands that you would breathe tensely in this highly dramatic or physical situation, you will have to. But then it is vital to know how to revert to relaxed breathing as soon as the camera cuts.

 Remind yourself how relaxed breathing feels. Sit back comfortably or, better still, lie down. Drape a hand on your stomach around your belt line and stop thinking about your breathing. Just listen to the sounds around you. After a few moments become aware of the rise and fall of your hand. You will feel that it is moving away from you a little as you breathe in, and going back towards the spine as you breathe out.

This is because, as you take a breath, your diaphragm – that great, strong breathing muscle – contracts downwards, creating a little vacuum that allows your lungs to fill, and your stomach muscles move out of the way so as not to impede its progress. When you breathe out, the diaphragm relaxes back up. That is when your outer stomach muscles take over, contracting in their turn to help squeeze the air out of your lungs. You will recognise that familiar, comforting rise and fall of your stomach just before you drift off to sleep.

Most people who haven't trained as actors or singers, when asked to take a breath, will breathe in reverse. They will pull their stomachs in on the in-breath. This is a 'fight and flight breath' or sometimes called 'clavicular breathing', and this probably happens because we don't normally have to think about breathing; it is an involuntary mechanism. If it were not so, thousands of people would die each night whilst watching *EastEnders*. So, when untrained people have to think about breathing, they default into a stressed breathing pattern.

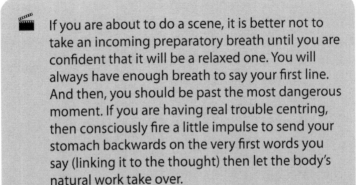

If you are about to do a scene, it is better not to take an incoming preparatory breath until you are confident that it will be a relaxed one. You will always have enough breath to say your first line. And then, you should be past the most dangerous moment. If you are having real trouble centring, then consciously fire a little impulse to send your stomach backwards on the very first words you say (linking it to the thought) then let the body's natural work take over.

You can check this movement by putting a hand over your stomach (your thumb should rest around your navel) and letting the breath out slowly for as long as you can on a 'Sh…' sound. You will feel your stomach flattening back.

Now put the forefinger of your other hand a few inches in front of your mouth. Making sure that your stomach is moving in the same direction (backwards), blow out a little imaginary birthday candle. It is one of those annoying ones that keeps relighting. Blow it out three times on each breath, making sure you recover by releasing your stomach muscles to let the breath back in. Keep your mouth open between puffs, as we do when speaking. You should be able to keep going until you stop because your stomach muscles ache. You should never run out of breath. If you do so, you are not completely releasing back to normal between puffs.

Now move your finger away from your mouth to the full extent of your outstretched arm. Blow out a candle at that distance. You will feel how much more your stomach moves.

All speech is normally on the out-stream of breath, which is why you feel your stomach go inwards as you speak. (I have observed that the Norwegians, strangely, do sometimes say a non-committal 'Ja' on an in-breath, but they are the exceptions that prove the rule!) The louder you want to be, the bigger this movement will become.

 Do the same work as above using a voiced 'Maa' instead of just breath. Make sure you are fully voicing and the quality of the sound is not 'breathy'. Because your vocal folds are now meeting, breaking up the airstream to create sound to which you are adding resonance to help the sound carry, you will feel less movement in your stomach area. But you should still feel movement to some degree and it should be stronger with the louder sound when your finger is further away.

We do all sorts of 'displacement activities' unconsciously to avoid the commitment of speech and action. Watch that you don't add neck tension, jut your chin forward or lift your shoulders before you speak.

 Become aware of your breath in your daily life. Does it change when you are under stress? Have you forgotten to breathe? Are you still holding your breath?

 Don't get into the habit of letting the breath out before you speak. You are simply buying yourself time so you lose the energy and impulse of the moment. 2.4

Recent research has shown that there are a few people who don't panic when they have an adrenalin surge in extreme situations. They stay calm and alert, like the American pilot who guided his airplane to safety on the Hudson River. So maybe there are a few lucky actors born with this ability to stay cool under pressure. But most of us have to learn how to do it.

The breathing and relaxation work in this workshop will help you to harness the energy of adrenalin and make it work for you and not against you. I recently watched an interesting experiment on television. The reporter had his brain wired up to a scanner and was then subjected to a large needle being inserted into the back of his hand. He yelled loudly, and the part of his brain which responds to pain lit up. He then went through a series of breathing and relaxation exercises with a hynotherapist but remained fully awake. The needle was reinserted and he smiled and said he felt only a little pressure. His brain now showed no activity in the region that had lit up before. Hypnosis and relaxation techniques have long been used in childbirth and pain management.

I am not suggesting that you act under hypnosis. You will need your adrenalin for energy. But I am suggesting that you use relaxation at home when filming is getting stressful. And that you continue to breathe without stress whilst you work.

2. Tics and Tensions

When we're not relaxed, our bodies try to dissipate the tension by these 'displacement activities' I've mentioned. For example, if, inwardly, you want to walk away from a situation, you may start to shuffle or rock or drum your feet. If you are nervous, you may lift upwards off your hips, which makes your trunk move slightly from side to side. Or you may develop a slight shake in the head or a tremor in your hands. Your eye may twitch, or a tic can show in your face. In close-up all these things are magnified. In a large cinema, your face may be blown up to fifty times its normal size on screen. Imagine how apparent these little tensions then become.

If you are in a tight close-up and standing on your correct mark but you shuffle or shift weight, your image on camera will go out of focus and they will have to do another take. The only way to combat all this tension is to stay at ease. But how do you do that with all that adrenalin streaming around your body? Again, only by making sure that the breathing is working in a natural and relaxed manner. That means having worked on it enough for the muscles to remember how to do it.

The great acting teacher Michael Chekhov said that an actor had to burn within, under an outer ease. This feeling of ease needs to be with you before you can start your work. Before going on set be sure to relax away the tensions of the day. If you have at least an hour before filming, you can lie down to do a full relaxation:

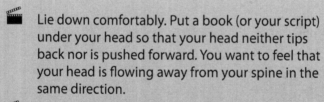

   Lie down comfortably. Put a book (or your script) under your head so that your head neither tips back nor is pushed forward. You want to feel that your head is flowing away from your spine in the same direction.

   If you wish, you can bend your knees upwards, with your feet flat on the floor to allow the small of your back to relax downwards.

   Go through your body, tensing and relaxing (muscles will only fully release if contracted first). Tense your toes – relax them. Tense your legs – relax them. Clench your buttocks – relax them. Pull in your stomach – release it. Pick up your hands, give them a shake and let them fall by your sides, palms upwards. Lift your shoulders off the floor, then let them go. Press them down into the floor, then release them. Screw up your face – relax it. Wiggle your tongue, then let it fall into a relaxed position.

▪ Really feel the weight of your whole body on the floor. Feel your shoulders widening, your back lengthening, your neck lengthening away from your back.

▪ Slide a hand onto your stomach. Forget about your breathing and think instead of the weight of your body and the sounds around you.

▪ If you prefer, imagine you are on a beach or in your garden or just about to sleep.

▪ Take your awareness to your hand and feel the rise and fall of your breath. Feel your hand rise to the ceiling on the inward breath and down to the floor on the outward breath. Breathe into your hand, increasing this movement.

If you don't have long before you go on set:

▪ Use the posture work from Workshop 1 so that you are standing in your neutral upright position of ease.

▪ Now shake your hands vigorously. Hop from one foot to another, shaking your feet. Blow out through relaxed lips (like the sound a horse makes blowing air).

▪ Then return to your neutral position. Check your knees aren't locked and feel the crown of your head rising to the ceiling.

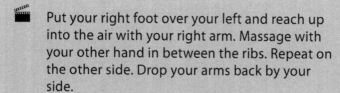 Put your right foot over your left and reach up into the air with your right arm. Massage with your other hand in between the ribs. Repeat on the other side. Drop your arms back by your side.

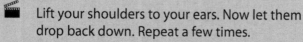 Lift your shoulders to your ears. Now let them drop back down. Repeat a few times.

Roll your head in a gentle half-circle then balance it back up, with your neck lengthening away from your spine and your chin parallel to the floor.

Now use this relaxing Qigong breathing routine called 'The Seasons'. 🔘 **5.1** When you get used to it, each step should flow into the next with no breaks between, the movements should be gentle and relaxed:

Spring: stand in the 'at ease' position – hold your arms loosely out, in front of you slightly bent, at waist level. Clench your fists lightly. Now let the breath out on a strong steady 'Sh...', raising your hands a few inches and bending your knees slightly. Imagine green shoots coming out of the earth.

Summer: straighten your legs, open your hands and draw your elbows back to your sides, with your hands at chest level, as the breath comes back in. Feel you are taking a deep breath of summer scents.

Autumn: put your arms back to your first position, in front of you but with the hands open, palms to the floor. Bend your knees as you let the breath out in a long gentle 'Sh...', dropping your hands a few inches as if they are the leaves falling.

Winter: let your arms drop to your sides as you straighten your legs, letting the breath in through your nose as if peacefully returning to your inner strength.
🎞 **5.1**

A few rounds of this are very relaxing. Finally:

🎬 Rub your hands together hard to make them warm, then place them across your upper chest. Shut your eyes, take in the warmth and let your shoulders relax and your chest soften.

🎬 Rub your hands together again, place them on your belly and breathe into the warmth.

🎬 Rub your hands together one last time. Place one hand on your belly and the other at the small of your back. Feel your power and strength.

On set:

🎬 Put your hand on your belly for a few seconds before filming begins, shut your eyes and imagine breathing into your hand.

🎬 Placing your hand over your belly during close-up can also help you to stay emotionally connected and help with the twitches that can shift you out of focus. (You can only do this if the position of your shoulders will match the wide shot because of continuity. 🎞 **4.3**) This is also great to do during vocal post-production work, when you are standing in a voice studio trying to lip-synch your words.

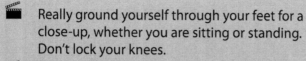

- Really ground yourself through your feet for a close-up, whether you are sitting or standing. Don't lock your knees.

- Make sure that you haven't lifted at the hips and hollowed your back, but that you are connected and aware of a relaxed breath before you begin. This will take tics and tension off your face.

- Now think what you want in the scene and focus on that and not on yourself.

3. The Connected Voice

A voice that carries no resonance carries no information about the speaker and doesn't engage the listener. This 'unsupported' voice is often not even as loud as it would need to be in life and so is as unnatural as using excessive volume on camera.

When the ability to have live voices on film arrived in the cinema, the sound mixer was king. Everything stopped for the soundman to adjust his microphone and fix the sound quality. Then post-production came in and gradually the importance of live sound was eroded. The irony is that the more sophisticated the sound department has become at providing post-production, the more this has devalued their work on set and the more it has devalued the role of breathing and voice quality in the minds of actors working in film. It is a vicious circle. Because actors aren't producing good, clear, intelligible sound when filming, more and more directors rely on ADR (Automatic Dialogue Replacement) or post-synching or looping. Some actors get so good at it that they claim to prefer it. And yet it goes against what acting is about.

Acting is interacting, reacting, and being in that moment. How then can this add-on sound be preferable? Of course there are times that it is inevitable – when planes have roared over a medieval set, a waterfall has drowned out the loudest voices or the director has insisted on the use of wind machines that sound like helicopters taking off on every shot. But there are many films where all the sound conditions were fine that still loop everything. A British director told me recently, 'I used to use original sound, now I much prefer ADR – the sound is so much more focused.'

Well, that's because the actors aren't giving him a 'focused' sound. They are using breathy, disconnected voices that don't convey anything. There is a current fashion for using such low, breathy tones that even the other characters can't hear. That is not being naturalistic. That is simply a current style and will be thought of at some future date as a very unnatural one. When you talk you are driven by an impulse, a need to communicate something. In life, if you said something to someone and they didn't hear it, they'd ask you to repeat it and you'd have to use a louder voice. And, as mentioned earlier, even if the dialogue has to be replaced in post-production for technical reasons, this initial lack of vocal energy during filming means the visual and aural do not match.

Of course, you don't want an unnaturally loud voice either. You want the voice you'd use in life in that situation. You need the right volume to communicate at that given moment – neither more nor less. Sometimes you may be asked to be a bit louder because of good technical reasons like a background noise that will be added on afterwards, like a steam engine, for example, or motorway noise. But then, in life, it would be there anyway. On screen you need an ability to keep a 'soundscape' in your head. For example, if there is dance music playing in the scene, it can be played during rehearsals but not during shooting as picture and sound are recorded separately. When you do the scene, there is silence, but you need to imagine that the music is continuing to play as you speak.

I worked on a film once with lots of young actors doing a scene that was set in a disco. The music would be played during rehearsal but as soon as we went for a take, the actors had to imagine the music was still there. They found it extremely difficult. They would start by speaking loudly but within a few moments, the levels had dropped back again because they felt a bit daft using so much volume on the quiet set. No matter how many times the director or I nagged them, they couldn't keep the volume up. Needless to say, that scene had to be done again for sound at a later date!

Sadly, as post-production becomes the norm, more and more films are simply using the live sound on set as a guide-track to dub to later. Ultimately, we may make television as they still do in Turkey or used to do in Spain. We will shoot all action mute and add sound on later – probably with different actors. Do we want that? I think it's time we honoured our heritage and were as conscious of the quality of our voices and our need to communicate on screen as we strive to be in theatre.

After all, our best movie and television actors are recognised and admired as much for their voices as for any other part of their acting skills. In many European countries, where they dub all their foreign films, they still find it is important to choose the same voice for a particular actor. So Clint Eastwood or Ralph Fiennes or Jodie Foster, for example, will be dubbed on all their films by the same person so that the voice is consistent, film to film. Even when it is not the original actor speaking, the voice quality is still an important part of the package.

Films are mainly about high-intensity moments or moments of great emotion. If the voice is not connected or 'centred' – that is, driven from the abdominal-diaphragmatic area – it does not carry emotional resonance. If we are not using a fully released voice in moments of high activity, the body will not look fully engaged either. When we lived a more physical way of life, people's voices were naturally 'connected up'. They were fully part of the whole body. But now, so many actors (along with the rest of us) are disconnected. They speak from the neck up. Consequently, we cannot believe they live the physical lives of their characters.

Because our larynxes are not fixed in place but suspended, when we get tense, we can hold them higher than they should be, which makes the pitch of our voices go up. If you gently hold the sides of your larynx (either side of your 'Adam's apple'), and hum up and down in pitch, you will feel your larynx moving up and down too. It is moving up and down inside your pharynx. Like any musical instrument, if you shorten this tube by holding your larynx high, your pitch will go up.

Here is a quick way of getting an idea of your natural relaxed pitch 🔊 **3.1.c**:

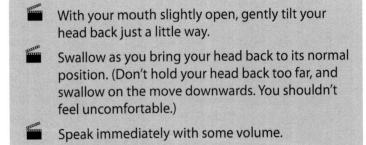

- With your mouth slightly open, gently tilt your head back just a little way.
- Swallow as you bring your head back to its normal position. (Don't hold your head back too far, and swallow on the move downwards. You shouldn't feel uncomfortable.)
- Speak immediately with some volume.
- You will often find your sound is lower and richer.

It is important to speak immediately with a connected voice – if you use a breathy tone, you will not hear the difference. To make sure your voice is not breathy, do this:

> Wag your finger as if you are telling someone off and say, 'Uh-uh, Uh-uh.'
>
> Now keep everything the same and say, 'One, two, three, four, five.' This manoeuvre helps your vocal folds to make full connection and stops the breathy sound.
>
> Now do the 'tilt and speak' manoeuvre again.

A lot of women hold their voices high from habit or social pressures. If you listen to female television presenters from the 1950s, you will hear their voices are higher pitched than presenters today. Then along came the sixties and the larynxes – and voices – dropped! Nerves also cause tensions here that affect pitch. Some men hold their larynxes too low. It causes strain to hold your larynx down; you want your larynx to move up and down, as it needs to, in a free, released manner. And you want it to revert, after speech, to its normal resting position without tension or constriction.

On set, you can get a similar releasing effect by simply sipping water between takes!

And whilst we are speaking of water, remember to keep the hydration going. Sets are hot and dry places, so drink lots of water. If your voice is tired at the end of the day, use steam to soothe it. Steam is the only thing that can reach your larynx. Anything you swallow gets sent down the oesophagus so you don't choke. In time-honoured fashion, you can put a towel over your head and breathe in steam from a basin of hot (not boiling) water or you can use an electric steamer. Or you can simply lie in a hot bath or use a steam room.

Using abdominal–diaphragmatic breathing makes the vocal tone more resonant and assists good vocal technique. It is the power source for the voice and directly affects the way the vocal folds work and all other aspects of voice use.

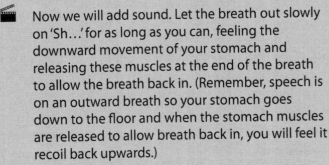

- Relax through your body again as described in the previous section, lying on the floor with your head on a book.

- Now we will add sound. Let the breath out slowly on 'Sh…' for as long as you can, feeling the downward movement of your stomach and releasing these muscles at the end of the breath to allow the breath back in. (Remember, speech is on an outward breath so your stomach goes down to the floor and when the stomach muscles are released to allow breath back in, you will feel it recoil back upwards.)

- In a rhythm of three beats, with a little extra strength on the middle beat, say 'sh – SH – sh'. Try to use up all your breath on these three beats by consciously using your stomach muscles to pull down to the floor on the outward breath on your gentle 'sh – SH – sh'. This is like a gym exercise for these muscles to remind them which way to go under stress – you won't use this conscious movement in real speech. Repeat ten times alternating between 'sh – SH – sh' and the voiced sound 'z – Z – z'.

- Turn onto your side, remove the book from under your head, rest your head on your outstretched arm and repeat this work. For some people, it feels much more natural in this position. As your breath goes out on 'sh – SH – sh' you will feel your stomach moving backwards towards the wall behind you. When you release your stomach muscles to allow your breath back in, it will move away from you towards the wall in front of you.

Do the same with voiced fricatives: 'z –Z – z', voiced 'sh – SH – sh' (like the sound in the middle of the word 'leisure') and 'v – V – v'. (This will make your voice sound instantly buzzier.)

Come to a sitting position and repeat this again.

Now come slowly up to standing position, being careful not to strain your neck. Bring your head up last. Go slowly – don't get dizzy.

Repeat the work, keeping your back straight and taking care not to lock your knees. **3.1.a**

Clasp your hands in front of you and shake out a sound.

Massage your face, bringing the flat of your hand from your jawline downwards, allowing your jaw to drop open. Chew vigorously with your mouth open for twenty seconds.

Rest a hand on your stomach and speak without working consciously from this area. You should still feel a gentle movement backwards as you speak. And you should feel your stomach muscles release forwards as the breath drops back in.

If your back is fine, bend your knees (to protect your back) and hang over from your waist, fully releasing your neck. Have your legs no wider apart than a normal standing position. Speak loudly and come up slowly as you speak, leaving your neck relaxed and bringing your head up last to its normal position. You should hear a new fullness and richness. (It is important not to let the voice change – as you get near to standing, you need to go on engaging your abdominal muscles.) 🪩 **3.1.d**

🎬 If you can't do the exercise above, drop your head onto your chest and roll it gently back and forth in a half-circle from one shoulder to the other (not backwards), speaking loudly. Then balance your head back into its normal position and continue speaking without changing the sound.

🎬 Taking the tension out of your neck and hanging over is also a really great way to free up your acting, although you can't do it in full hair and make-up!

If you are new to voice work, you may find this extra resonance strange, but it is worth remembering that we don't hear our voices as other people do, so we are more aware of change. Our ears are in the wrong place, so we only get the bass. To check better how you sound from outside:

🎬 Hold your hands outstretched behind your ears, making 'fans' of them. Then speak. Now you will hear the 'top' in your voice and you will get a clearer idea of what other people receive.

It's just as important to warm up and cool down vocally for screen work as it is for theatre. At the end of a long day:

Gently sip some water.

 Hum up and down from top to bottom of your range. Or use a gentle '...ng' sound to 'siren' up and down. This stretches your vocal folds. Just like stretching after jogging!

A connected voice has the 'ring of truth'. We believe you because we sense, in a deep subliminal way, that you are at ease with yourself and connected to your emotions.

4. Emotional Release

We have so many phrases about feelings that relate to our abdominal area and the solar plexus – 'I was gutted', 'gut instinct', 'I felt it in the pit of my stomach', 'my stomach knotted with anger', 'my stomach turned over', and so on. Around this area, many sympathetic and parasympathetic nerve endings cluster. That is why we feel sensations that we associate with fear or anger in our stomachs. Why we ache there with loneliness. Or feel a zing of excitement. Actors need immediate access to feelings, and if the breath is dropping into this area and the throat is open, there is a direct channel between emotion and communication.

We also feel emotion in our laryngeal area – 'I was choked up', 'I had a lump in my throat', 'I couldn't breathe'. This is because this area, too, has a large number of these nerve endings. Consequently, the voice is a sensitive indicator of emotion. You know when you talk to a good friend on the phone whether they are unhappy or not, whatever they say.

Above the vocal folds lie the false vocal folds. They are the 'gatekeepers'. They start to shut when adrenalin races through the body or if you are ill or tired. This is because they protect your airway. When you eat or drink, they close along with the vocal folds, so that you don't choke.

If they narrow the airway, they restrict the breath flow and the voice sounds creaky. This also shuts you off from your emotional centre. The creaky voice is common among teenagers when they want to seem cool and to hide emotion, it is the voice of old people who are too tired for emotion and it is the voice of all of us at the end of a long tiring day! (I think of it as the vocal equivalent of folded arms.) Of course, this voice quality can also cause damage if you are speaking with volume.

Here is a simple exercise to put you in touch with these tiny constrictors (and constriction is restriction!) 3.1.b:

> Put your hands over your ears and breathe through your open mouth. Hear the breath, like the sound of an 'h' on the inward and outward breath, and then make it silent. You should feel a slight widening inside your throat. You should also feel more movement in your abdomen as you breathe.
>
> Take your hands away and speak, keeping this tiny internal stretch. Your voice should sound richer.

You may possibly feel more vulnerable too because you have opened up that emotional channel to your solar plexus area. This retraction of the false vocal folds is what singers automatically do when they are about to sing. We also do it when we laugh or cry.

There is a recent system called 'Alba Emoting' developed by a neuroscientist, based on working through breath patterns to release emotion. I attended an intriguing workshop by Rocco Dal Vera, who is a certified instructor. By following patterns of breathing, posture and facial expression, six basic emotional states are explored and a seventh is used to restore the actor to a neutral state. By breathing to the pattern of the emotion, the body steps into the state of that emotion and the mind follows.

As an actor, you can work from the outside in or the inside out. The most important thing, however, is that you are breathing from the abdominal–diaphragmatic centre and your throat is open. Then you have a direct access to your emotions. When you commit to the specifics of the situation, you allow the emotions to happen naturally.

If you have to feel deep emotion, you can use this simple breathing exercise:

- Sit on the floor and rock forwards, letting the breath out on a sustained 'Hah'.
- Keep rocking and breathing and start to release the breath through a voiced 'Aah'.
- Lengthen the sounds and feel you are emptying all your feelings through this sound. (Be careful not to become hysterical – keep it structured.)
- Gradually return to normal breathing, feeling where the emotion was churning.
- Trust the work and return to the scene you are working on.

If you cut this abdominal–diaphragmatic area off by holding your stomach muscles clenched, the likelihood is that you will start to 'manufacture' emotion. Your face will start to work much more than it does in life and you will start to 'show' us what you feel. On film, this will appear untruthful.

5. Inspiration

When we think, we breathe. 'Inspiration' means both the act of breathing in and having a brilliant idea. As each new impulse drives us, so the breath is energised to give that impulse words and actions. If we don't honour the breath each thought needs, our impulses are ironed out and the work becomes dull and muddied.

In life, we don't know when one thought will give way to another or when we will stop talking. As each new impulse drives us, we take a breath to give voice to that thought. Because actors have learnt lines or see the words on the page, they often signal that there is another line coming. They tip the tune of the line up at the end. They run the thoughts together. They forget to breathe.

By honouring these breaths, each thought will seem freshly minted and spontaneous. Breath is so linked to thought and feeling that we can sense how someone is feeling by the way they breathe. As we take a breath with each new thought, everyone thinks, and therefore breathes, in a different rhythm. As we get excited our breathing gets quicker; as we get more relaxed our breathing slows down.

By paying attention to the breath as the thought changes, we can start to see how the role thinks. If someone speaks with lots of short sentences, it indicates their brain is racing fast, whereas long sentences are driven by a strong thought that has to be taken to the end before breath is drawn.

The voice teacher Cicely Berry has an exercise that you might want to try before you have learnt your words. First, walk around your room, reading your script, and at each punctuation mark, change direction. This puts you in touch with the 'rhythm of thought'. You could also change chairs, pick up a different object, or touch something in the room on each comma or full stop. After all, punctuation is simply the way a writer signals a new thought.

 Now try a variant. Improvise your thoughts as you in the role, and change direction every time a new thought occurs to you.

By observing the punctuation, we get into the head of the person the writer created. By doing the same thing with your own thoughts, you are training yourself to stay in the moment of the thought and not to jump beats. To allow one thought at a time.

Finally, if you are not breathing, you cannot listen. You mustn't know what the other person in your scene is going to say either. If you keep breathing, you will really hear – instead of pretending to do so.

6. Vital Energy

Breath is the energy that drives us through life, and gives life to each thought and action. If nerves make us breathe clavicularly, in the 'fight and flight' mode, then our lungs are not properly filled and our muscles are starved of vital energy. Without the breath driving the voice with the energy needed, the words are flat and lifeless. If the false vocal folds are constricted so that the voice 'creaks', then there will be no energy driving the sentence.

Equally, if breath escapes through a chink in the vocal folds on voiced sounds, we will have a breathy quality, which can sound unconfident or uncommitted. If breath escapes before we speak, like a sigh, it results in a loss of energy. The words cannot fly. They will sound depressed and under-energised. If we 'miss the moment', breath and thought will be disconnected. ⏺ **2.4** Through control of our breathing, we can harness the adrenalin so that instead of blocking us, we are able to channel it into vital energy.

> 🎬 Don't take a locking breath in before you begin. Just feel the impulse to speak and respond to it on the instant.
>
> 🎬 Don't let the breath out before you speak. You are buying time and 'missing the moment'.
>
> 🎬 Use a full released voice at the volume you need to reach the other person in that situation. Keep your throat open. Need to communicate.

7. Empathy

It is a strange phenomenon that when we are in tune with people, we start to breathe at their pace. In a theatre, an audience will hold its breath with the actor at a tense moment or breathe faster with excitement or give a sigh of relief when all is well. On screen, too, we get caught up with the emotional life of the character and breathe in sympathy with them. If breath and emotion are not matching, an audience will feel it as untruthful.

When people are in agreement with each other or feel close, they mimic each other's movements. When they are angry with each other or disagree, they choose a different posture or a posture that 'blocks' the other person. If you watch chat shows on television involving several people in discussion, you can see this very clearly. If you've ever seen the famous clip of the very drunk Oliver Reed taking part in the late-night television show *After Dark* (take a look on YouTube!), you will see the other participants shutting off from him very clearly. They lean back, cross their arms and ward him off by any posture they can find. It is compelling viewing!

This mimicking or deliberate mismatching of breath and movement can be used to create empathy or tension in the performance. If the roles are in tune with each other and the actors breathe together, the resulting scene is compelling because we feel the real relationship between characters. If, on the other hand, the roles are at odds with each other, you will sense their different patterns of breathing.

Empathetic breathing can only happen if you are relaxed and allowing your breathing to respond to each other and to the 'as if' of the situation naturally. If you are so tense you hold your breath, so will everyone else. And this may not be at all right for the situation!

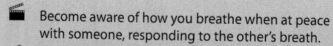

Become aware of how you breathe when at peace with someone, responding to the other's breath.

In day-to-day life, practise matching your breath to others. Use the same rhythms of speech. Practise mismatching by choosing a different pattern of breath and speech.

This work will both help you to respond naturally with easy breathing when you are in empathy with the other role and to keep your own patterns when you need to.

Ongoing Posture Work

It is hard to breathe properly unless your alignment is good. It is worth watching how you sit and stand in daily life and making an effort to adjust it on a daily basis. Don't brace yourself or hollow your back to attempt to sit upright. Find your 'sitting bones' and sit relaxed but upright with your neck lengthening out of your back and your head balanced on top. Your neck should not be tense when you speak.

If you have a partner to work with, try this game to find the 'dantien' or 'hara', where your power lies and how it controls posture, balance and strength:

- Stand in front of a partner. Snap your fingers in front of their eyes to get their attention and ask them to concentrate on their forehead. Now gently push them on the shoulder and they will immediately come off-centre and lose balance. (Don't let them fall over!)

- Check their posture. Ask them to really feel the floor with their feet, unlock their knees and feel the crown of their head rising to the ceiling (as in the neutral 'at ease' position).

- Now, standing next to them to allow them a clear view, gently talk them through their body, releasing tensions. Tell them to make their face soft and to release any tension there, to relax their neck, shoulders and chest tension. Then hold your hand a few inches in front of their abdomen and ask them to imagine breathing into your hand. Now tell them to keep this centred breathing as you try to push them again and that they can resist you, but only as much as they need to.

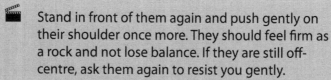 Stand in front of them again and push gently on their shoulder once more. They should feel firm as a rock and not lose balance. If they are still off-centre, ask them again to resist you gently.

When they do that, they will feel that where they are controlling their balance from is the central area around the solar plexus – the 'dantien' or 'hara'. They will become really aware of that connection. They will also feel how connecting with this area takes away extraneous tensions and helps posture.

Now ask them to do this game with roles reversed!

You can also do the posture work (outlined in Workshop 2: 'Instant Posture') with a partner.

(It's important to check your partner has no neck problems before you do this!) Stand behind your partner and find the hard bony area at the base of their skull. With one hand gently holding your partner here, lift their head just a few millimetres skywards and ask them to walk forwards feeling 'tall'. See that their chin is parallel to the ground. Then let them find this position themselves.

You can go further. Stand behind your partner. Take both hands and pinch an inch of skin between your fingers just above their shoulder blades. (It can be a little painful!) Now lift your hands (and their skin) a few millimetres and get them to walk a few steps. Then they can find those supporting muscles themselves. (Make sure they keep their shoulders down.)

Have you noticed how wonderfully straight a toddler sits? They are using their back muscles to support themselves. We forget to use these muscles fully because we lean on desks, slump on sofas and slouch over steering wheels. If you are to look convincing in period films, you definitely need to find these muscles again!

Shoulder Workouts

It is worth noting that as well as shoulder and neck tension blocking your performance, it can block you physically too. When an actor tells me that she or he feels uncomfortable and restricted in movement – the 'What should I do with my hands?' syndrome – I check their shoulder alignment as well as the thought processes. If you brace your shoulders back (and men are more inclined to do this), your arms cannot move freely. Try it and you will see what I mean. Equally, if you collapse your upper chest, moving your shoulders forward (this affects more women than men), this will also lock your arms. It affects your voice too, and is a common reason for voice strain.

I have spent whole movies simply massaging my actor's shoulders down and magically, their acting has improved! Here are some magic ways to take tension out of your shoulders:

 Lie on your side with the arm underneath you stretched out at right angles. Now move your upper arm at right angles across your body so that your hands meet. Now gently massage your lower hand with your upper hand, keeping your arms straight – as if you were massaging cream into your hand. Now start stretching further and further beyond the lower hand onto the floor in front of it, and then back up the arm until your whole body is rolling back and forth. Repeat on the other side.

Lie on your back and imagine a light switch on a cord above your head, just a little out of reach. Reach one hand up, turning your hand outwards to reach the cord – stretch once, give up and let your arm fall back by your side. Stretch again, stretch harder, fail again and let your arm fall back by your side. Try a third time – stretch. Finally you can reach to switch off the imaginary light and let your arm fall back to rest position. You should feel that shoulder now lies flatter to the floor. Repeat on the other side.

Stand easily with your knees slightly bent and reach right round your body with your arm, twisting your waist in three little twists and turning to look as far behind you as possible. Let the breath out 'Sh – Sh – Sh' as you do this. Come back to normal position. Reach again as you breath out again on 'Sh – Sh – Sh' and try to see further round. Come back to neutral. Twist round the same way a third time. Come back to normal. You will see further each time. Repeat on the other side.

Stretch your arm out at right angles and press against an imaginary wall. Push against the wall and let the breath out on a sustained 'Sh...' as you do this. Let your arm drop back by your side. Repeat three times on each side.

Now gently twist your shoulders from side to side, letting your arms swing loosely across your body. (Like a twelve-year-old standing by the garden gate in the summer holidays, wondering what to do next!)

If you are with a partner, get them gently to hold your arm bent behind you with the back of your hand resting on your spine. This opens up the area behind your shoulder blade. Get them to massage you with a dozen hard strokes downwards in this space behind the shoulder blade. Then they can hold your arm at right angles to your body, give it a little shake and let it drop. Your shoulder will drop down noticeably. Get them to do the other side to even you up.

The Actor's Toybox: Physical/Psychological Games

The Pavlov's Dog Effect

Our minds and bodies are absolutely linked. I always use the 'lemon test' to bring this home to actors:

 Imagine a lemon on your kitchen surface at home. See its yellow, waxy shape. Feel its bumpy surface.

 Now take an imaginary knife and cut your lemon in half.

 Pick up one half of the lemon and hold it close enough to smell it. Take in that clean citrus scent.

 Now quickly put the imaginary half-lemon into your mouth and suck hard.

I guess that you felt more saliva in your mouth or felt your lips pucker. Now ask yourself this: if your imagination of a lemon could actually bring saliva into your mouth, how can you doubt that your memories and emotional recall will bring real physical changes? Tests have been done on athletes who recall their races whilst wired to machines that can check their pulses, blood pressure and hormone levels. Their pulses increase, blood pressure goes up and identical hormones are released into their bloodstreams as the ones they release when they actually run.

When you watch the DVD accompanying this book, you will see people telling stories of things that happened to them and you will see the colour come to their cheeks, their breathing change and their bodies echo the physicality that they experienced. They will speak with the tone of voice in which other people spoke to them, show us geographically where things were, and, above all, see and feel again what they experienced first time round. ⊙ **1.1, 2.1, 2.7**

You can't cheat with this. You have to find a way in rehearsal to have experienced what your role felt. You have to have some muscle memory of the experience and the pictures and sounds in your head. Then you must trust this work and deal with each moment as you would in life. That is the purpose of this rehearsal work – to build that unconscious iceberg lying beneath the surface of your role – to add to and to twist the viewpoint of your own inner life – to find the physical life that you in the role leads and has led. You also have to find joy and exhilaration in this work – even if you in the role are dealing with harrowing experiences. It is meant to liberate you rather than constrict or torture you. It allows us to deal with painful or terrifying experiences in a healthy way, just as the work we create allows the audience the same cathartic release. You are going to *play* the role – you are going to *play*. That is why I call them games rather than exercises.

Improvisation as a Rehearsal Tool

You need to start by exploring the scene as if it were real life, not worrying about how it will be shot or limited by the constraints of the camera. Most actors know about improvisation, but not necessarily the most useful way to use it as a rehearsal tool. They tend to improvise the scene itself. That doesn't often help you to learn much more, unless the language is very dense or you are moving a period piece into a modern setting to help you to relate to it more easily.

The best way to use improvisation is to enrich your imaginary life and make you more specific about it. Use it to make relationships deeper or give you more connection to the life you lead. Use it to wake up the child in you to believe fully in the world you must inhabit as your role. 🎧 **2.9, 3.3**

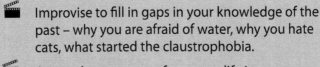 Improvise to fill in gaps in your knowledge of the past – why you are afraid of water, why you hate cats, what started the claustrophobia.

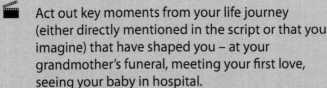 Act out key moments from your life journey (either directly mentioned in the script or that you imagine) that have shaped you – at your grandmother's funeral, meeting your first love, seeing your baby in hospital.

Improvise scenes to build relationships – like having your older sister bathe your knee, doing your daughter's hair, sorting your husband's wardrobe, choosing your wedding dress.

Act out any stories or anecdotes that you recount in the script so that when you tell them, your energy will go outwards, moving between the pictures and sensations of your past and engaging with your listener. You won't be trying to 'see' them for the first time.

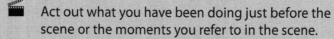 Act out what you have been doing just before the scene or the moments you refer to in the scene.

Release your imagination by playing the scene whilst changing the role and the circumstances – be a child, a politician, an alien who has never seen Earth before, an Elizabethan courtier, and so on.

Not all scenes are naturalistic. Don't be afraid to let your imagination take you to places you yourself have never been or to use language and ideas you would not normally use.

Lie on your back, relax and whisper (no voice at all!) the scene very, very slowly and let your imagination and visions take you where they will.

Physical Metaphors

I work through the physical whenever I can. One of the traps for an actor is thinking too much. By that, I mean thinking as the actor rather than the role. A predominantly head-driven approach to preparation can simply confuse the actor and there is the danger of trying to remember this preparation work in the moment of doing, which can make the work heavy and loaded with obvious subtext.

When I am directing, I like to use physical metaphors to clarify what drives the scene. Here are some examples of what I mean, using scenes from Shakespeare's plays – as you'll probably be familiar with the context.

Take the scene from *Romeo and Juliet*, where the Nurse has news of Romeo but is teasing her charge by pretending she is too tired and out of breath to give Juliet any information about her lover. You could run the scene with the Nurse doing everything to avoid eye contact whilst Juliet tries desperately to make her look at her to get the information she wants. This could involve running, circling each other, hanging on to each other, tickling, offering chairs – until the Nurse gives in. Then the scene can be played properly but the physical work will have created the emotional undercurrent to the scene.

In the first scene of *King Lear*, when Lear is dividing his land amongst his three daughters, he might stand in the centre of the space. Goneril, Regan and all their followers make a circle around him. Cordelia is on the outside of this circle. As Goneril and Regan try to outdo each other in descriptions of their love, Lear tries to reach Cordelia, but the circle of arms prevents him from doing so. Cordelia tries to reach Lear, but eventually gives up, saying, 'I cannot heave my heart into my mouth.'

Hamlet might be physically pulled like a tug-of-war by different characters at different moments in the play. Or he might be walking an imaginary tightrope whilst they are trying to shake him off by yelling lines at him. Or he might be a drowning man clutching at them as they slip through his fingers – trying to decide whether to take action or not, whether to live or not.

You can use these physical metaphors with a partner to find a quick connection between you. Or to pinpoint the drives of the scene. For example:

 Lost Love: if you have to play a scene where both partners no longer love each other (or are trying not to show that they still do love each other), hold each other quietly, just absorbing the warmth of each other's bodies. When one of you claps your hands, pull apart immediately and do not look at each other again. Then play the scene and you will have uncovered what you once had together that is now missing or still longed for. But you have found it in a fundamental way through experiencing it. **3.4**

Motherhood: if you haven't had a child, you need to find a physical metaphor for motherhood. Try imagining the baby as a part of yourself – first in your belly and then as your own limb. Then as the child grows, start to feel this limb stretch away from you on a piece of elastic. Sometimes it pulls far away and then bounces back. Sometimes you pull it back. Eventually the elastic stretches so far that it snaps. A part of you has been severed. **3.5** No one has explained motherhood better than Sylvia Plath in these beautiful lines from 'Three Women: A Poem for Three Voices':

> ...it is as if my heart
> Put on a face and walked into the world.

 Status Work: your scene may involve two people, each trying to dominate the other. Working with your scene partner: every time you feel you have scored a point, jump up onto a chair or another (safe) high point. Every time they score a point, jump off. If they land a verbal body blow, fling yourself to the floor. This will pinpoint your mental activity through your physical moves.

Subtext: every time you feel you are telling the truth, look at and move towards your partner. Every time you are lying, look away and take a step away.

Dance your needs, sing your thoughts, paint pictures of your past, pack your life in cardboard boxes, dig your goals into your garden, search for your hopes like seashells on a beach, run from the ghosts of your past, find the still deep pool of where you are or search a dark forest to find where you've come from.

There are no rules. Whatever physical metaphor you use will be governed by your vision of the action and influence what actions you take. But whatever you choose, you will commit to it with every fibre and not just 'think' about it. You will come out of your head and into the physical life of the role.

Psychological Gestures

Michel Chekhov called the archetypal movement that is the physical metaphor for the driving need of a role, 'the psychological gesture'.

"" So we may say the *strength* of the movement stirs our will-power in general; the *kind* of movement awakens in us a definite corresponding *desire*, and the *quality* of the same movement conjures up our feelings.

Michael Chekhov
To the Actor

I was once using this work with an actor when he said that the psychological gesture he had found was the equivalent of his 'super-objective'. I hadn't thought of it that way before but I agreed with him. Stanislavsky's super-objective – the driving need for the whole journey of a role – can sometimes be hard to uncover by merely thinking about it.

It is hard enough to know what one wants in one's own life and the super-objective can appear to change through the course of the script. But by using this physical work, the actor is instinctively uncovering the spine of the role – the deepest drive. Like Michael Chekhov, I prefer using psychological- gesture work to thinking too much about the super-objective. That way, the actor doesn't get tangled in thought but finds the primary drive and need of the role through the body.

When an actor first works on the hidden subtext and drives, the scene can get a little heavy as the actor wants to 'use' these hidden currents in the work. By crystallising them into a movement and a phrase, it is easier to bury them and fly freely on top of the work, as we do in life. Life is interesting because of its ambiguities and you don't want to iron them out.

During a workshop, I was working with the scene from the end of the film *Doubt*, written by John Patrick Shanley, where the Mother Superior has suspected the school priest of molesting a boy and has had him removed. She is telling a younger nun that he won't be coming back and that she has no doubt he did it. The actor playing the older nun played the scene very coldly, as if she had no doubt of the man's guilt, and this made her very unfriendly to the younger nun. When she found her psychological gesture, she realised she was actually filled with doubt about what she had done but couldn't admit it. When she went back to the scene, she trusted the subtext and didn't need to show it. The dialogue played very lightly and the relationship with the younger nun was very natural. But at the end of the scene, left alone, the close-up revealed clearly, and with enormous vulnerability, the depth of her doubt as to whether she had done the right thing.

Many fine actors, like Jack Nicholson and Anthony Hopkins, use psychological-gesture work as part of their preparation. Here is how to find a physical metaphor for what drives your role, either for the whole part (the 'spine') or in any given scene. This is my version of psychological-gesture work, and it adds the spoken word to reinforce the physical work. Once you have found your movement, speak your need aloud or use a phrase from the script that reinforces the drive of your movement and keep repeating it whilst you do the movement. 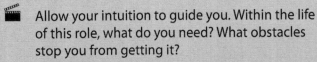 **3.5**

> 🎬 Allow your intuition to guide you. Within the life of this role, what do you need? What obstacles stop you from getting it?
>
> 🎬 Allow these drives and feelings to enter your whole body and – using strong, non-naturalistic movements – find a gesture that embodies what you want and how you feel. Involve your whole body using a simple, strong movement.
>
> 🎬 Keep experimenting until you find some movement that feels right and seems to 'connect you up' with what is driving you in the role. Keep it simple, clean and strong. Discard and change your movement as many times as you need to until you instinctively know you have found the one that is right for you in this role at this moment.
>
> 🎬 Keep playing with the gesture until you feel you have connected with the life of the role. The movement should not represent your surface action but uncover what is driving you to take that action. Repeat this movement over and over at least ten times.

- Now speak your 'want' out loud, whilst you do the movement. Say it in the form 'I want...' or 'I need...' The words will come out of the movement. Keep refining the words until you feel that the movement and the words match. (Alternatively, you can choose a key phrase from the script that you feel reveals the core of the role.)

- Using a fully connected voice and the strong, all-encompassing movement, repeat at least six more times.

- Now bury the work completely, deep within you.

- When you go back to your scene, use only the conscious thoughts and drives of the role – and trust that the work is done.

- This will give you a deep driving need within you but enable you to be light and subtle without feeling the need to show us the subtext or get 'heavy' with the text. If the scene has no subtext, it will power any action truthfully.

- Sometimes a tiny shadow of the work or 'echo gesture' will creep into the work and enhance it. But do not try to find these – they will appear naturally if you simply follow your impulses and work naturally.

- Repeat the words and movement in the pure non-naturalistic form whenever you need to re-enter the role after a gap in filming. You can also do this if there is any post-production work later.

- You can use this work for any role, but it is especially useful for one that is powered by a deep need or concealing a secret or that you find difficult to connect with.

Emotional Props

Emotional props are another kind of physical metaphor. They provide a subtext to your inner world. You will see them used around you in life. The other day I saw a man and a woman walking down a train platform in London. They were American and therefore far from home, and it was obvious from their conversation that they didn't know each other very well. As they talked, the woman constantly twisted her wedding ring round and round. Was she just feeling vulnerable or was she starting an affair? Was she recently widowed or simply missing her husband? I certainly wanted to know the story behind her use of that personal 'prop'.

A scene where a woman cleared the nursery of her dead toddler's clothes and toys would need no words. The way she touched the baby's clothes and held the toys that had been played with so recently would tell us everything about that loss.

When you dust your mantelpiece, you will linger over some objects and as you touch them, memories will flood back to you. There is a scene in the film *Miss Potter* (2006), where a friend and sister of Beatrix's dead fiancé brings her a picture as a present. It is a picture Beatrix (Renée Zellweger) had painted and given to her fiancé on the night he proposed. The way in which she unwraps the gift and holds it to her tells you all you need to know about that relationship and the loss she has suffered.

You have to be careful not to overuse emotional props, but often, like the example above, they are already built in to the scene. If you choose to add one and do it judiciously, we can learn more about your inner life. One of the most famous examples of this in film history is the scene in *On the*

Waterfront (1954) where Marlon Brando picks up one of Eve Marie Saint's gloves that she has dropped and puts it on, whilst talking to her coolly. The intimate way he handles the glove shows what he really wants from her. (If you've never watched this scene, you can find it on YouTube.)

If you've really done your homework on your world, the objects that you handle will acquire familiarity and significance and some, like life, will become imbued with your emotional life.

'Gestus'

Out of our inner feelings come external movements. Bertolt Brecht called this physical embodiment of an attitude a 'gestus'. A pregnant woman really does touch or hold her stomach. It is a kind of recognition and protection of the baby inside who has entered her inner life before joining her outer world. A vulnerable person may rock themselves in a deep need to re-enter the safety of childhood. Feelings of anger, frustration or fear will result in physical manifestations that give away these inner needs. We may clench a fist, tap a table or pull at our hair.

As well as the conscious 'emblematic' gestures that we make, such as a 'thumbs-up', a 'V' sign or the 'phone me' symbol with thumb and little finger held up, we make spontaneous underscoring gestures to our spoken language that are read and understood subconsciously by other people. Sometimes these movements give away more than our words. Interestingly, if you point to the left but say 'right', people will correct your verbal mistake, knowing that your gesture is the truthful version.

We use 'iconic' gestures to describe an actual object – for example, the thickness of a tree or the arc of a passing plane.

'Metaphoric' gestures give ideas a physical shape and form. They give away the speaker's attitude to what they are saying and are the official classification for those 'echo' gestures left by your work on the psychological gesture. You may clutch at a mental tree like a drowning man when you feel lost, or part imaginary mists to see more clearly, or show the geographical placement in your mind's eye for right and wrong, past or present. As mentioned in Workshop 2, you may tap or press your upper chest with your open hand or your knuckles to 'push down' emotion that might overwhelm you.

'Deictic' gestures point and show actual directions, and 'beat' or 'baton' gestures emphasise the rhythm of your spoken words or the order of your thoughts. They emphasise your speech and act as if you used a yellow highlighter pen or underlined words to show us what you feel is most important in your sentence.

Gestures can be pantomimic and represent actual objects and actions or show what we feel about circumstances, feelings or ideas, or place them in precise geographic or spatial localities in our mind's eye. (⊙ 3.7 Watch Georgia describing her dive!)

We all use these unconscious gestures, regardless of our race or language. That is why having your hands in your pockets or behind your back will be read as a disinclination to engage with others. If you, as an actor, feel too inhibited to use these natural gestures, your performance will not seem spontaneous or truthful. You have to give yourself permission to use them. The director Jonathan Miller says that his only task with actors is 'reminding them of what they know and have forgotten, and getting them to forget what they never should have remembered in the first place'.

In other words, you need to remember to do what you would do naturally as a human being, and forget to do what you think you 'ought' to do as an actor! You have to give your-self permission to follow your impulses and to communicate as freely and naturally as you would in life. If the thought 'What should I do with my hands?' occurs to you – you can-not be thinking or trying to get what you want hard enough or seeing the pictures in your head. If you are, your hands will take care of themselves.

Every day, our movements and gestures reveal our deepest drives. We all have an inner rhythm of our own, bound up with these thoughts and needs. This shows in the way we express ourselves by movements – whether we dab with our fingers or make elegant sweeps with our whole arms, whether our gestures tend to go outwards towards the world or inwards towards ourselves. Each human being has a unique tendency to be fast or slow with speech and movement, heavy or light, twisting or direct. In our desire to express ourselves, communicate our feelings and obtain what we want, we constantly reveal these inner motions. They reflect our attitude to the world and how we deal with it.

Patterns of Energy

One of the ways that the Hungarian choreographer Rudolf Laban categorised human activity was into eight 'efforts': glide, float, dab, flick, wring, slash, thrust and press. Each of these movements is sustained or sudden, light or strong, and direct or flexible. For example, the act of floating is sus-tained, light and flexible. You could float through actual movements such as waltzing or you could float mentally – metaphorically. Someone could float through life, making no decisions, letting the wind blow them where it will. When you yell in anger you could describe that sound as 'thrust'. It is sudden, strong and directly aimed at someone or something. We combine all these movements, both physical and metaphorical, into our lives, but have a default tendency to gravitate to one of these patterns of energy. We may float through life or flick at it or constantly wring with guilt. Our voices, too, will glide or dab at words. You may slash or press or thrust to get what you want or repel what you do not. By exploring them all, you widen your choices and increase your awareness.

The following games are loosely based on Laban's eight efforts (having explored them with, amongst others, Jean Newlove, who was Laban's assistant and worked with Joan Littlewood in bringing Laban's work to the attention of actors in Britain), but I am not using his work in a 'purist' way. These games are to increase your freedom with physical metaphors. I have kept Laban's descriptions as they are widely known.

Have fun with the following patterns of movement. Try the movements in lots of different ways and contexts; do them larger than life; add voice using the same patterns. This is an excellent way, too, to address particular voice habits, like glottal stops. Think of gliding through the words – don't allow any dabs. You can change from one effort to another in a moment. Try taking a poem or a monologue and playing each line with a different effort, using both your voice and a movement to capture the feel of that effort. Use voice and movement together to glide, float, dab, flick, wring, press, slash and thrust your way around the room.

Use this work in an imagistic way. The examples below are just to get your imagination going. All good actors use a variety of rhythms, tempo, light and colour in their work, so my film suggestions are just an overall impression that the performance leaves me with (most of these performances can be found as clips online).

1. Glide: sustained, light, direct

A galleon, a society hostess, skating, ironing, roller skates, charm, grace, a swan.

Grace Kelly as Tracy Lord in *High Society* (1956), Greta Garbo in *Queen Christina* (1933), Christopher Lee in *Dracula* (1958), Fred Astaire dancing in anything!

2. Float: sustained, light, flexible

A feather, a balloon, flirting, the clouds, as the wind blows you, autumn leaves.

Vivien Leigh as Blanche DuBois in *A Streetcar Named Desire* (1951), Marilyn Monroe as Sugar Kane in *Some Like It Hot* (1959), the plastic bag dancing in the wind in *American Beauty* (1999).

3. Dab: sudden, light, direct

A chicken, finger-wagging, staccato, drumming your fingers, tapping, stammering.

Jack Lemmon as Felix in *The Odd Couple* (1968), Laurel and Hardy, Leonard Rossiter in the Cinzano Bianco commercials.

4. Flick: sudden, light, flexible

A hair toss, shrug, deflect, throwaway line, flicking ash, finger snap, the Charleston.

Henry Winkler as the Fonz in *Happy Days* (TV), Shirley MacLaine in *Irma La Douce* (1963), Miss Piggy of the Muppets, John Hurt in *The Naked Civil Servant* (TV), John Travolta dancing in anything.

5. Press: sustained, strong, direct

Arm wrestling, the club bore, bullying, hectoring, pushing a car uphill, interrogating.

Pauline McLynn as Mrs Doyle in *Father Ted* (TV) and her famous phrase 'Go on, go on, go on…', Michael Caine in *Get Carter* (1971), Jeremy Paxman interviewing Michael Howard on *Newsnight* and asking him the same question twelve times.

6. Wring: sustained, strong, flexible

Hand-wringing, guilt, shame, obsequiousness, writhing with embarrassment, pain.

Gene Wilder as Leo Bloom in *The Producers* (1968), Alec Guinness as Fagin in *Oliver Twist* (1948), Peter Lorre as Dr Adolphus Bedlo in *The Raven* (1963).

7. Thrust: sudden, strong, direct

A punch, command, yell, kick, 'Stop!', 'No!', a hurtful comment, a slammed door.

Charlie Chaplin as *The Great Dictator* (1940), Robert De Niro as Jake LaMotta in *Raging Bull* (1980), Spencer Tracy as John J. Macreedy in *Bad Day at Black Rock* (1955).

8. Slash: sudden, strong, flexible

Sword-fighting, conflict, reinforcing, fencing, laying down the law, clearing a path.

Charlie Chaplin (again!) as *The Great Dictator* (1940), Gérard Depardieu as *Cyrano de Bergerac* (1990), Uma Thurman versus Lucy Liu in the final duel of *Kill Bill: Vol. 1* (2003).

You may have also noticed that all the direct efforts (glide, dab, press and thrust) involve outward interaction with the world. They involve the will, decisions and are a direct consequence of the impulse. They are about reaching out or imposing your will on others. The flexible ones (float, flick, wring and slash), on the other hand, allow something to come between the impulse and the execution – a subtext. They deflect, defend, bluster, parry, protect, turn inwards or prevaricate.

As well as using the effort that might be a clue to your role, working on these will help you to recognise your own habitual tempo and style, as you will find your own preferences the easiest to do. In order to increase your range for different roles, you need to work with those that you find difficult. I find so many actors tend to dab these days, that when actors ask me what they should work on, it is invariably gliding or floating. If you work with a thrusting energy for power or anger, it is imperative that you centre yourself and don't allow your head to push forwards. As the really strong efforts can be vocally challenging, do a vocal cool-down at the end of your work.

Circles of Need

This is an amazing game for pushing boundaries, removing all decisions about 'how to', building relationships and being in the moment. It is the fastest way I know to get real depth in a scene and is like three weeks' rehearsal in ten minutes. You can use it with a partner or on your own. (🎧 **3.8, 5.5** Watch Marion and Remco 'circling' before returning to the scene they are to play.)

Circling with a Partner 1

 Find a phrase that expresses your need in relation to your partner in the scene – for example, 'I want you to forgive me', 'I need you to confess your sin', 'I want you to show me you love me', and so on.

 Your partner also chooses a phrase that embodies their need towards you.

- Now forget the context of the scene, and using all the available space and complete physical freedom, repeat these phrases to each other, making sure you keep trying different ways to get your needs. You can do anything provided you don't hurt each other or wreck the room!

- Stick only to your decided phrase. Do not use any other words.

- At first, consciously try a different action each time to get what you want – for example, flirting, pleading, bullying, loving, consoling, teasing, and so on. (This is just to get the exercise going – soon you will just follow instincts and respond to your partner.)

- Don't give yourself time to prepare between repetitions, go with the impulse.

- You are allowed genuine silences that come out of the need, and you can go out of order if you want to repeat the line again before your partner's.

- Don't let yourself off the hook. Go past the point where you can't bear to repeat any more.

- After a while, by a kind of osmosis, you will find yourself drawn back into the situation of the scene.

- When that happens, obey the context – look at each other, touch each other and gently whisper the wants a few more times or do anything that the scene demands. But do it quietly without any sense of 'pushing'.

- If your needs change dramatically within the scene you are to play, you can repeat this game again with the new 'wants'.

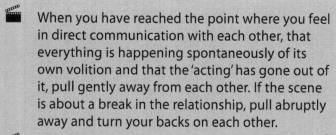 When you have reached the point where you feel in direct communication with each other, that everything is happening spontaneously of its own volition and that the 'acting' has gone out of it, pull gently away from each other. If the scene is about a break in the relationship, pull abruptly away and turn your backs on each other.

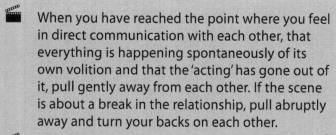 Now return to the full text and play out the whole scene.

Circling with a Partner 2

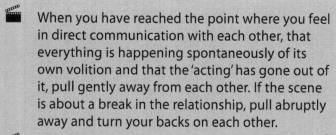 Find a short, pivotal line from the actual text you are to play and one for your partner.

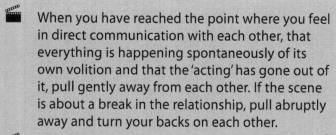 These can be phrases from anywhere within the dialogue and although they should be from within the same emotional beat, they don't have to follow directly on.

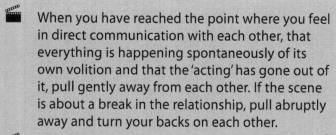 Now follow the same directions as in version 1, but using the phrase from the actual text.

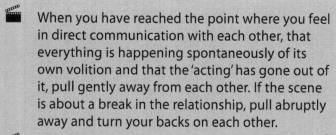 You can find a phrase from the text for each time the beat changes and work your way through the whole scene.

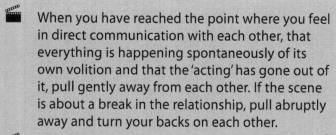 Now return to the scene as written and play it out as it happens of its own accord.

Circling Alone

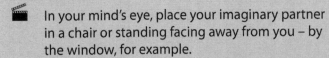 In your mind's eye, place your imaginary partner in a chair or standing facing away from you – by the window, for example.

Know exactly who they are and what they look like in great detail. Or make them someone you know.

Imagine that they never respond or look at you (for whatever reason).

Find what you need from them and a phrase to embody it. Or take a key line from the text.

Forget the context of the scene at first and use the whole space to work in.

Keep repeating your phrase to your imaginary partner.

Don't plan how to do it the next time, just respond to your instincts.

Allow the fact they do not react to increase your need to reach them.

Try a different way each time to get your need.

Eventually you will feel yourself drawn back to the scene. Stand still and whisper your phrase a few more times.

Shut your eyes and then let the work go. It will add depth when you play the scene without you trying to remember it.

Circling for Specific Needs

- You can connect to a relationship by repeating the name of the person many times.

- Visualise the person and keep calling, whispering, saying their name and needing something different from them each time.

- End by whispering their name slowly with your eyes closed a few more times.

- You can do this with any significant names of people or places or specific words, to make them so natural to you that they become part of your role's history.

- If you have difficult words or even jargon or scientific names, you can use this device to make them familiar to you and their use second nature.

Mask Work as a Rehearsal Tool

We all have a 'social mask' which we wear to cover our insecurities and cope with the world. We smile too much, or crinkle our eyes, or purse our lips. Our features harden and set, and we begin the lines that will etch themselves into the mask of our old age.

Working with actual masks might seem a strange rehearsal technique to use in preparation for screen work, but I have been using them for many years in my workshops and when coaching film actors, and they can be an invaluable part of the rehearsal process. They replace our social masks, leaving us free beneath them to experience performing without fear. 💿 **3.10**

I use 'neutral' masks in neoprene made by Jonathan Becker and based on those devised by the sculptor Amleto Sartori for Jacques Lecoq. No masks, however, are ever really neutral, and even masks that appear identical will turn out to engender slightly different results. My current masks are brown, larger than a human face and do not allow you to speak but, over the years, I have experimented with many types of masks. White, neutral masks can be a little dead and the *Commedia dell'Arte* leather masks and the Victorian cardboard ones, whilst still being marvellous to experiment with, can be too character-oriented for first beginnings. You want to find a mask that, when you first look at it, doesn't seem to have its own story to tell.

You can make your own masks out of cardboard or even a brown paper bag. You can choose to cut a hole for your mouth, although true neutral masks are full silent masks. (And, even with a half-mask, you have to prepare very slowly for speaking.) Of course, you do need eyeholes to see through and a band to hold it to your head. You don't want to paint it with any kind of face or decoration that would take it away from neutrality. If you want to be more professional about your mask-making, Toby Wilsher's *The Mask Handbook* (Routledge, 2006) has a section on how to make masks and some online links to mask-makers. Toby Wilsher is a mask theatre director and co-founder of Trestle Theatre Company. Reading his book a few years ago, I was amazed to find him, too, comparing mask acting to screen acting in its ability to show private thought. I thought I was the only person to have seen this strange connection!

I work with these neutral masks, as the actor is less likely to 'lead' the mask into caricature, but all masks will be liberating as they release you from your habitual disguise and seem to open the way to your inner self. Oscar Wilde wrote that if you give a man a mask, 'He will tell the truth.' Jacques Lecoq maintained that neutral masks help an actor to strip away old habits, enhance the actor's presence and give a blank page on which to build. They are a great way to break long-held patterns of movement and energy.

I have studied mask work with many practitioners over the years and in many different mask genres. As I need to work fast for film rehearsal, I have had to shortcut some of the more ancient traditions of mask work. I cheat and use a mirror at the beginning and end of the work to allow the actor more instant feedback.

These are the effects that I observe in my workshops. The eyes become all-important. The mask seems to 'distil' movement and strip away any that is extraneous. The body becomes relaxed and open, and movement becomes economical. The mask slows you down. The actor will see, hear and be aware with a new innocence. The actor's energy goes outwards and towards the world and other people. Instead of worrying about their own performances or nerves or trying to get feedback and reassurance that they are 'feeling', the masks really watch, play and echo each other. There is teamwork, they play a lot of mirroring and copying games. They develop bonds and gangs. They are driven by strong primary needs. They are not ambivalent. They look rooted. They show clarity of thought. They react spontaneously in the moment without preparation – they don't know or need to know what happens next. They sense status and play out power games. They have real relationships with each other. They have a sense of their own strength. They invent a story and an identity. No wearer of the mask ever looks the same and even the same wearer looks different each time.

At recent workshops, I asked the participants to give me a word or phrase for their experience within the masks. Here are some of their remarks:

I didn't know what would happen at any moment

I felt cleaned afterwards

curious

invisible

I was so in love

aware

shy

stillness

I felt totally rejected

not the person you know

incredibly moving

safe

surprised by my aggression

excited

could use my body in any way

concentrated

a new creature

vulnerable

ridiculous but happy

frightened by the possibilities

overwhelmed by feelings

every feeling was magnified

every action was gigantic

freedom

someone taking you over

everything I saw and touched was new

couldn't control what I felt

Most of the participants felt they had touched something new inside themselves or released some previously held constriction. A few felt claustrophobic or negative. No one was neutral towards the experience. The observers reported these reactions:

they looked so free and strong when they took off their masks

really engrossing

everything is distilled

connections establish and keep changing

people change personalities

they were together and open

really notice eyes

I didn't know the words to describe what I saw

their eyes are very expressive

you see what drives them

they are driven by strong, basic needs

I saw the essence of the people

the group dynamics were fascinating

androgynous but sexual beings

they disappear into a new being

Because the mask allows no human expression, people are less inclined to 'show' emotion or to use the social mask of smiling or frowning. They are in touch with their instinctual reactions. When they take the mask off, their faces are clean, their bodies straight and open, their eyes dance. I ask them to look around at each other and the observers without changing anything, and to feel their own power. For some people, this will have been a turning point and an immense discovery of themselves. For me, seeing the transformation before their social masks slip back on, it is as if a veil has been lifted. It is an extraordinary and moving moment. (⊙ **3.10** You really see this openness when Daniela, Massimo, Nicole and Alexis take off their masks.)

I think true openness is a rare quality in an actor. We move through life trying to avoid pain and rejection, trying to be liked. We have to be brave when we are not, appear to like things that we do not. To hide our feelings, to show feelings we don't have and to avoid feeling at all; to be too close to people for comfort; to be alone when we need to be loved. Small wonder that we learn little social habits, expressions and movements that harden into the masks with which we deal with the world. Both men and women build carapaces against the world, but women appear especially prone to this social mask. Perhaps we women need more guile, artifice and subterfuge to survive.

All this was strongly brought home to me once, many years ago, whilst watching Adrian Lester play Rosalind in Cheek by Jowl's *As You Like It*. I was struck by the directness of the performance and suddenly reminded of the young Vanessa Redgrave who shared this quality when she played the part. And I realised how rare it is. Women tend to disguise themselves under a veneer of sweetness or elegance or charm. They are seldom simple and open. Masks can allow you to be brave enough to drop your guard.

Jacques Lecoq wrote in his book, *The Moving Body* (Methuen, 2002), 'The neutral mask, in the end, unmasks.'

Using the Mask Alone

 Find a full-length mirror. If you don't have one, then put the largest you can find on a table so you can see as much of yourself as possible. You will often find something suitable in a bathroom or on the inside of a wardrobe. You can work in any room.

 Sit on the floor with your back to the mirror. Take the mask in your hands, try to clear your mind and just look at it and receive anything from it that occurs to you.

- Now put the mask on. There is an absolute rule here. Once you inhabit the mask (or it inhabits you) you must not speak. If you need to adjust it a little, do, but if you need to interact with the world as yourself you must remove the mask.

- Breathe gently with your eyes closed for a moment (sometimes masks are uncomfortable and claustrophobic, and breathing is difficult so take time to adjust). Then stand in front of the mirror with your eyes open.

- Stand relaxed and at ease and breathe slowly. If you want to adjust your clothing or hair, do it gently and go back to your neutral relaxed pose.

- Stand for a few moments simply looking at yourself and absorbing what you see.

- Very slowly and deliberately start to make a few tiny movements. Allow the mask to 'guide' you. You may move just a shoulder or tilt your head or lift a hand.

- Gradually become braver and 'feel' what the mask wants you to do. Try not to impose on the mask or allow yourself to become caricatured or consciously 'act' some odd creature. You are looking for your inner-self to channel through the mask. (Although some would argue that it is the mask channelling you!)

- When you feel confident, turn away from the mirror and start to explore your surroundings.

- If you are working on a role, you can pick up objects you would use in your role or think the thoughts of the role.

- You may also experiment with the psychological gesture of the role whilst wearing the mask.

- You may be surprised to find that it is hard to continue down the path you wish. You have to allow the mask to lead you.

- When you have played for a while, turn back to the mirror and become neutral and at ease again.

- Remove your mask as gently and cleanly as you can (be careful you don't catch your hair in the rivets as this can hurt and spoil the moment for you!)

- Don't change anything. Simply look at yourself and observe.

Breaking with some traditions, I use the same neutral masks for group work and find they can interact with each other.

Using Masks with Others

- Ideally, everyone in the room should have their own mirror, but it is possible to take turns with one large mirror.

- Sit with your backs to the mirror/s, take your masks in your hands and observe them, taking what you feel from them.

- Put the masks on in as neutral a way as possible and just breathe and stay relaxed. You can adjust them as you need to for comfort. But you must not speak or interact with each other yet.

- Now go to the mirror. If you are taking turns, wait quietly until your fellow mask has left the mirror and then take your place in front of it.

- Take time simply to observe yourself and breathe naturally. (Sometimes it is hard work breathing in a mask and you need to overcome any tension this brings.)

- Now start to make small movements. Keep adjusting these until the mask seems to be leading you.

- When you feel at one with the mask, turn away and observe your environment.

- Now observe your fellow masks. Take your time with this.

- Working very gently at first (until the masks take over of their own volition), start to interact with the other masks through tiny movements.

- As the masks lead you on, allow yourselves to play. This may sound strange, but in practice it simply happens. I have never given the masks any instructions; they simply evolve games, battles and love affairs.

- When you have played for a while, go back to neutral. Stand in front of the mirror. Gently take off your mask, taking care not to catch your hair.

- Quietly look at yourselves and absorb your openness and power. (If you are taking turns with the mirror, don't take your mask off until you are in front of it.)

- Now look at each other without the masks, keeping the body grounded and open and resisting the temptation to reinstate your 'social mask'.

Structured Group Work

 You can, if you wish, impose a game on the masks. 'Grandmother's Footsteps' works very well. One masked actor stands with their back to the group. The group have to tiptoe up and touch him or her. 'Grandmother' keeps turning to catch any movement from the encroaching masked actors. Any actor caught moving has to go to the back of the group. Other children's games like 'Musical Chairs', 'Oranges and Lemons' or 'Pass the Parcel' also work well with masks.

 You can use your psychological gestures if working on a role and pursue your 'needs' with other masked actors. It doesn't matter if you are not all in the same scenes. This can bring new insights into your preparations, but don't expect your masks always to want what you want them to want! Masks can be anarchic and hard to direct from within or without.

The psychiatrist Carl Jung felt that masks released the collective unconscious, and there is this sense of the mask releasing you from the personal and leading you towards a bigger, more archetypal sense of reality. There is also a link to Meisner's work on immediacy as the masks operate in the here and now. They make you aware of the semiotic whole of where you are and what you are feeling. And, because there is nothing subtle or social about masks, when you wear one, you allow pure, basic impulses to drive you.

How does this work enrich your private rehearsal? Well, I don't think you can see it as a logical or linear progression to your role. It is a way to put you in touch with your posture and habitual movements and to change them. It is a way to 'play' your way into the role without censoring yourself. The sense of profound release from the day-to-day mask that we carry around can be enormously liberating, as can the power you tap in to by trusting your instinct moment to moment. It reminds you not to 'decide' what to do next. And maybe, just maybe, some wonderful, unexpected insight that you had in your mask will reappear in your work when you least expect it.

Chakras, Secondary Centres and Archetypes

Chakras (or what you might also think of as 'secondary centres' or archetypes) were first mentioned in Workshop 2: 'Recipe for STAR Quality'. Here is a game using a simplified idea of chakras. You should do this work light-heartedly – it is not a scientific pursuit or a deep exploration of chakras, but another way to play in order to find different energies for your role.

 Take a line from the script and say it, imagining you are speaking from the lowest point in your body – from the bottom of your feet. These have become your 'secondary centre' or 'base chakra'. Now add an imaginary spear to wield – you are now a warrior. Your voice will instinctively drop in pitch and you will feel strong and grounded.

 Take the same line again and imagine you are using only your sacral or groin area with which to speak. This is the 'sacral chakra' – the area associated with sexuality. Have fun – exaggerating a movement forward from your hips as you speak. Try saying the words 'I love you' from this area. If you use only this centre, and it is not combined with the 'navel', 'heart' or 'head chakra', far from being sexual, you will become the archetypal fool.

You are in the realm of Greek satyrs with attached phalluses! You will probably separate out your words and they will become staccato and robotic.

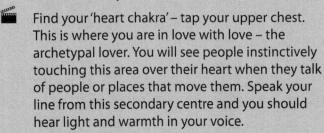 Find your 'heart chakra' – tap your upper chest. This is where you are in love with love – the archetypal lover. You will see people instinctively touching this area over their heart when they talk of people or places that move them. Speak your line from this secondary centre and you should hear light and warmth in your voice.

Purse your mouth and make it your secondary centre. (It isn't one of the chakras.) This is a sensual area – where you taste, kiss (and also flatter!). If you speak your text imagining you are speaking from your lips, you may feel sensual or simply manipulative or deceitful. But it will change the quality of your voice, your rhythm and inflections.

Tap your forehead and try to say 'I love you' as if you are speaking from there. Your thoughts are more likely to engage with your mortgage or the prenuptial agreement than your desire. This is where we spend most of our lives, sorting day-to-day practical problems, thinking and analysing. If you say your text whilst imagining it is coming from your 'head' centre, it will become practical and direct. Inflections will iron out and your speed will probably quicken.

Now imagine a centre on the top of your head or even above it, and speak from there. This is the 'crown chakra' – traditionally a spiritual and visionary area, but also where you might focus if you are under the influence of drugs or hallucinating. You might find your voice becomes light, airy and breathy as you speak. Your pace will tend to slow down.

Finally, place your hand on your solar plexus or 'navel chakra' – your primary centre. People hold or clutch at this abdominal area when they deal with difficult emotions. This is where we instinctively feel truthfulness and sincerity are rooted. This centre is known in Sanskrit as the 'manipura chakra', and its element is fire. All your energy and impulses 'fire' from this main centre. It is your powerhouse and provides the 'ring of truth' in what you say. Finish by speaking your text from this primary centre. It is your most important one as an actor.

You can experiment with mixing different secondary centres within the same role. If you were playing Joan of Arc, for example, you would have to be rooted from your primary centre but also work from both the warrior archetype or 'base chakra' and the visionary 'crown chakra' as well. This would automatically pull you in opposite directions from this primary centre – use this antagonistic pull to fuel your energy and your turmoil. Looking at it another way, Joan is torn between two needs – to fight for her country and beliefs (warrior) and her need to find spirituality (crown) – she is torn between her pride in her prowess and her humility.

If you are in a mismatching chakra or secondary centre for executing a task, the results will jar or even be comic. It's like adding a subtext that's not relevant. If I were buying a pair of shoes, for example, I would certainly be operating from my 'head chakra' ('I'm a size five or six…'); I could be in my 'heart chakra' ('Oh, I love those blue shoes…'); but I'm unlikely to be in my 'base chakra' unless I was fighting to get those shoes in a sale. And if I asked for the shoes from my 'sacral chakra', the assistant might run away rather fast!

Using this imagistic idea of chakras or secondary centres can awaken your imagination about a role in a new way. It is not to be used prescriptively, but only as another way of opening up new choices and breaking habitual vocal and emotional patterns.

The Animal Inside You

The great French director François Truffaut once said, 'An actor is never so great as when he reminds you of an animal – falling like a cat, lying like a dog, moving like a fox.' Basing your role on an animal, with the physical freedom that evokes, is a time-honoured approach. This doesn't mean that you won't be still be you, but in imagining yourself with an animal's drives and physicality, you will be released from your everyday tensions and habits, and enabled to explore new territory.

You can use this work simply to limber up and explore new possibilities. When I worked with drama students, I used to ask them to choose animals they felt were furthest from themselves, but, strangely, these animals would often have very similar patterns of movement to the students themselves. Then I would ask them to choose the animal furthest removed from the first animal they chose. Only then would they find new patterns and rhythms of speech and movement.

If you are using this work for a specific part, it is important to choose the animal that feels right for the role and you may have to experiment with several. When choosing your creature, don't forget birds and reptiles – or it might be an insect. I recently directed a scene involving a drug dealer; the actor playing the part decided to work on a spider. Drawing his clients into his web proved a powerful catalyst for his performance.

Don't try to become the creature from the outside. Instead, try to think like the animal. What do you want? What senses do you use to survive?

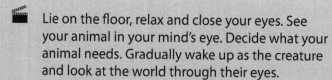

Lie on the floor, relax and close your eyes. See your animal in your mind's eye. Decide what your animal needs. Gradually wake up as the creature and look at the world through their eyes.

Now start to move around pursuing what you want. Don't try to become the animal from the outside, just feel you are using the senses the animal would use, the rhythms, the attitude. If this leads you to similar movements or posture, fine, but you don't have to be too literal. You are looking for the 'essence' of the animal – how you feel within its imaginary skin.

When you find something that feels helpful, distil the movement into a psychological gesture and repeat it a few times. Then allow yourself to acquire the human characteristics of speech and say what you want aloud. Finally, allow yourself to stand on two legs, and become more and more human.

Now bury the creature deep within you so that only you know it is there.

By exploring these physical extremes, you will find the stillness you need when filming. You will stop 'trying' and trust the wellspring of your inner power. You may also find a bravery to encompass the physicality of your role. If, for example, you find sexuality difficult, finding the panther – or the raging bull – within you may release it. If anger is hard for you without constriction or tears, you may want to tap into the force of a pit bull!

Triggering Emotions

Doing some work on your emotional memory and triggers can be useful as emergency back-up for tricky moments. This is not the same as substitution work. You will not be using your remembered scene during your performance. You need to do trigger work *before* you begin shooting, not during it. The triggers have a Pavlov's dog effect – just as imagining that lemon will make you salivate, so finding a trigger for tears, anger, etc. will provide the same response. For example, if you are working on tears:

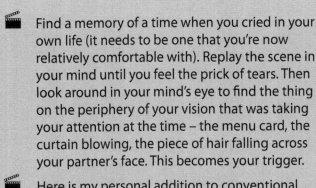

- Find a memory of a time when you cried in your own life (it needs to be one that you're now relatively comfortable with). Replay the scene in your mind until you feel the prick of tears. Then look around in your mind's eye to find the thing on the periphery of your vision that was taking your attention at the time – the menu card, the curtain blowing, the piece of hair falling across your partner's face. This becomes your trigger.

- Here is my personal addition to conventional trigger work: if you can't feel enough emotional response, speak the words you couldn't speak at the time – 'Don't leave me', 'I still love you', 'Don't die on me', etc. This usually provides an instant emotional release and the tears flow.

- Now forget the work. Half an hour later, flash up your trigger in your mind. If you feel the prick of tears again, you have found a useful trigger.

- You never need to go back to the memory again. You simply flash up the trigger to instantly feel a reminder of the original emotion. I don't recommend you dwell on triggers during the scene, but flash them up to connect with the feeling if you need to. Triggers get stronger with use. I consider them a kind of 'Elastoplast' to use only in an emergency. Think of them like priming your canvas before you begin to paint – then be in the moment of the brushwork and colours of the scene.

 You can find a trigger for tears, fear, safety, confidence, anger or happiness. Happiness is the hardest as it is seldom unalloyed. And if it is, you may still feel nostalgia when you return to the present!

Sensing Your World

What senses do you use differently or more strongly in this role? A sailor's eyes will be used to studying far horizons, a diamond dealer will see money crystallised through a lens, a lover will pick up clues in their beloved's face. A tailor will feel cloth differently, a farmer will run soil between the fingers and know what the crop will yield, a surgeon will be expert with delicate tools. A perfumer will use the sense of smell to make a living, decoding it into top, middle and base notes in a form of synesthesia. A doctor will recognise the smell of decay, a spice merchant will live with the scents of the East in his nostrils. The cook will savour a meal, tasting each subtle nuance of flavour, a child will test life with its tongue, a drug dealer may use taste to check for quality. A musician lives in a world of sound, rhythm and harmony, a mother seeking a lost child will strain to hear their voice, a trapper will hear the slightest rustle in the bush. If you are blind, your sense of hearing and touch must have become more acute. If you are deaf, you will live by sight and feel. The percussionist Dame Evelyn Glennie cannot hear her instruments, but plays barefoot so that she is acutely attuned to their vibrations.

I once worked with a mature actor who showed absolutely nothing in his face. He had to 'work' hard to allow thoughts to change his expression. I found this so unusual that I dug into his background. It seems that he had come to acting late in life and had spent the first thirty years being a psychiatrist – making sure that the patient on the couch saw no reaction in his face to any personal details that were revealed! The life you lead affects the way you react to the world, and you need to react as the role does.

Waking Up the Senses

 Take off your shoes and walk around your room. Now imagine you are walking on sand, in cold water, in mud, on hot stone, over brambles. Put your hands in an imaginary bowl of water. Let the water change to cornflakes, to snow, to rose petals, to sand, to ice, to treacle, to glue, and back to water.

 Imagine you are from an alien planet. See our world for the first time. Really notice things in detail. Try to work out what they are for. See the world with an innocence, a wonder at its beauty, a repulsion at its ugliness, a humour at its idiocy. Touch things for the first time. Taste things. Really experience the world around you. (These games became an important part of my work with Milla Jovovich on her role as an alien in *The Fifth Element* in 1997.)

Shut your eyes and sit outside in your garden or on a park bench for a while. Then open your eyes and look around you. The colours will be stronger, the shapes more distinct. Better still, wear a blindfold and earplugs and get a friend to guide you around outside. After twenty minutes or so, take off your blindfold, open your eyes and remove your earplugs. You will be amazed by the intensity of light and sound and will experience a short spell of really seeing and hearing afresh.

 Remember a room you haven't been in for at least five years but you know well. Imagine you are showing someone around it. Start by coming in the door. What kind of door is it? Show them around the room. What's on the bed? What colour is the carpet? How is the room lit? What particular book do you remember on the shelf? What time of year is it? What do you see out of the window? And so on. Finally, shut your eyes and stand in the room. What temperature are you? What do you hear? What do you smell? How do you feel? If it is a strong feeling, what trigger would bring this room and the feeling back to you? There you have a bonus point! You have done a sense-memory game and found a trigger. 🎧 **3.6**

This sense and memory reconditioning is vital for all our work in film, television, radio and theatre. But especially on camera we can see clearly whether you are really alive in your world. Although you can cheat all the technical aspects of movie-making, you cannot cheat the lens in the subtleties of thought and feeling.

For further reading, I recommend Michael Chekhov's *To the Actor* (Harper & Brothers, 1953) on psychological gesture, Uta

Hagen's wonderful book *Respect for Acting* (Collier Macmillan, 1973) for triggers, and Jean Newlove's *Laban for Actors and Dancers* (Nick Hern Books, 1993) about Laban's efforts.

Brain Games

We appear to use different processing styles with the two halves of our brain, but our knowledge about this is changing all the time. We now know that it is not as simple as the left side being logical and the right side being creative, though it appears we do perceive more details with the left half and the broader picture with the right. Some scientists claim that we use the left side of our brains for decoding language, grammar, word production and logical thought, and the right side for processing intonation and emphasis. The research is ongoing but the two sides do appear to be complementary – so by 'waking up' the connections between them, we can ensure that these two sides interact and 'talk' to each other more efficiently. Here are some workouts for your brain and body coordination.

 Put the forefinger and thumb of your right hand together, and the little finger and thumb of your left hand together. Now 'walk' your fingers by pressing each one in turn against your thumb. Your left hand will go through your fingers until your thumb and forefinger are together, and on your right hand, your thumb and little finger will be together. Then walk them back again. Make sure they finish where they started. You will find it quite hard to keep your fingers going in different directions. You will be inexorably drawn to touching thumb and forefinger on each hand. This is great for physical as well as mental dexterity – and a great way to kill time at a bus stop!

- Stand 'at ease', drop your head and release your jaw. Turn your head in a half-circle one way and then a half-circle in the other direction. Lift your head (by lengthening at the back of the neck) into the normal position. Now rest your head on one shoulder and nod twice to the opposite big toe. Then rest your head on the other shoulder and nod twice to the opposite toe. Now gently turn to look to the right with your head and then to the left. Look straight ahead. Now turn your head to the left but keep looking straight ahead as long as you can, then finally bring your eyes to the left. Now turn your head back to the centre, leaving your eyes looking left as long as possible. When you have to, take your eyes to the centre. Now repeat this on the other side. Now look to your left with your eyes and then follow with your head. Look to the front with your eyes and then bring your head to the centre. Look to the right and then turn your head. Look to the centre and then bring your head back to its normal position.

- Put your right hand out in front of you. Draw an imaginary figure of eight in the air. Make your figure of eight even and large. Draw five more figures of eight. Then do the same with your left hand. Now reverse the direction. This is a great 'wake-up' that clears the brain.

- *Gathering the Chi*: stand at ease with your legs slightly bent. Put your hands one on top of the other over your abdomen. As you breathe in, extend your right hand out to your side (arm slightly bent), palm up, as if you are gathering the air. Now take your hand round in a half-circle to just above your head and down in front of your eyes to your abdomen as you breathe out. As you are nearly at your abdomen, release your left hand out to your side as you breathe in and then repeat your circular action. You should never leave your abdomen without your hand on it for more than the briefest of moments. Do about twelve rounds. This Tai Chi exercise is a great way to start the day.

 This next idea is recommended by neurosurgeons! Do fine motor movements with the hand you don't usually use. By that I mean, if you are right-handed – brush your teeth, write, unscrew your water bottle, use your knife, dole out your vitamin pills, and so on – with your left hand. If you are left-handed – use your right. If you are ambidextrous – lucky you!

Nodes

Here is a group game for directors, but actors will benefit too. A long time ago, I used to go to workshops with the playwright David Mowat. We would write scenes from our lives. These scenes have to be no more than half a page long about a life-changing moment still sharp in the memory. David used to call them 'nodes'. The scenes can contain only dialogue that you believe was actually spoken and contain only the people in them that you remember being there. We did these scenes live, but I've adapted the idea for camera and it works very well.

 Write your scene in advance. Don't worry about ages, the actors can play toddlers or grandmothers, bridesmaids or ministers. Remember, be rigorously truthful and don't write more than half a page.

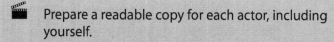

- Prepare a readable copy for each actor, including yourself.

- You have ten minutes only to cast your scene from the group and to give each player a thumbnail sketch of who they are, where they are, what they want (or seemed to you at the time to want), what they did and any circumstances surrounding the scene. You need to give them as much specific information as you can.

- You can rehearse a couple of times. The scenes are so short that the actors will more or less know them straightaway. You are allowed to give further instructions to match the scene closer to the one in your head, but you can't move your actors like puppets, and you can't tell them how to say the lines – only let them know what intention they had and what physical actions you saw them do.

- You can then adjust the scene a little technically to be able to shoot it – but without losing your sense of the truthfulness of the scene.

- Then you film it. Now play it back for the group. What you see on the screen is your new past!

When you watch it back you are looking for a truthful essence of your life. It is quite spooky to see these moments from your past – but they cease to be subjective. They have been transformed and transfigured by the creative process.

The benefit for the director is that, by being this specific and trying to match the pictures in your head, you learn how to instruct actors with the same specificity and to give them intentions rather than end results. You also learn to let go and allow the scene to acquire its own life. Make sure you set it up as it happened in life first, before you adjust it for the camera. If you set it up for the camera first, it will have no life. And you will find a few nudges here and there are all you need to film it. This game is also a great way to get an idea for a short film.

The benefit for the actors is that they get to play real, whole human beings in all their quirkiness and ambiguity through specific direction. Also, they will be released from worrying about their performances as their main desire will be to truthfully inhabit the writer's world. Which is what we should all be doing anyway!

 **Now watch Workshop 3 on the DVD.**

Workshop
4

Through the Eye of the Camera

Workshop
4

Filming the Script

❝ Film as dream, film as music. No form of art goes beyond ordinary consciousness as film does, straight to our emotions, deep into the twilight room of the soul.

Ingmar Bergman
The Magic Lantern

Film is an extraordinary medium. It allows us to see in a focused and precise way. The way in which a shot is framed, the tempo with which it is cut or the music that accompanies it, forces us to observe in the particular way that the filmmaker decrees, and provides the atmosphere to engender certain emotional responses within us. This is why an actor has no responsibility to provide any extra help for the viewer over and above the needs of the performance itself. You must not 'colour' your performance to show us it is sad or explain to us why it is funny. If you simply act and react truthfully, we will understand the story. Katharine Hepburn once said, 'If you give an audience a chance, they will do half your acting for you.'

It is salutary that, if you flick through television channels, you can spot the subtle clues of body language and voice that let you know whether you are watching an actor on a script who is trying to 'make it interesting' or someone talking about their real lives.

We have also become sophisticated viewers and have learnt about film grammar. This was brought home to me many years ago when my mother retired back from Africa where she had spent thirty years without a television. She was an intelligent woman, but it took her ages to understand what was fiction and what was documentary, who was an actor and who was not. We don't realise how expert we have all become.

We can differentiate between a real chat show and an ironic one, like *Knowing Me, Knowing You with Alan Partridge* or *The Mrs Merton Show* (both on TV). We know Dame Edna Everage is a character played by Barry Humphries, and that the grand stage actor Nicholas Craig is the alter-ego of Nigel Planer. Most viewers (though, strangely, not those he interviews!) can spot Sacha Baron Cohen behind his characters, such as Ali G, Borat or Brüno. We can understand we are watching satire and not a documentary with *This is Spinal Tap* (1984), *Best in Show* (2000) and *For Your Consideration* (2006). And although the film *Wag the Dog* (1997) and Damien's exploits in the television series *Drop the Dead Donkey* might suggest that not all news footage is as real as we imagine, we can, usually, see the difference between genuine news footage and what has been re-enacted.

Sometimes filmmakers intentionally break film grammar, like Buñuel or the French directors of the *nouvelle vague* ('new wave') who used jumpcuts and direct address to the audience, or they break with conventions by lulling us into thinking we are in one genre and then move us into another

– like *Wars of the Roses* (1989), which begins as a romantic comedy and then kills off the protagonists at the end. Or *A Knight's Tale* (2001), which incorporates deliberate anachronisms of time, place and music, like a track by the rock band Queen in a medieval setting. Or, like Lars von Trier, they experiment with what film can and can't do. The impact of these films relies on our understanding of film grammar so that we feel a shock when the rules are broken.

But it must be the director who decides whether or not to disturb the audience. As actors, we have to be careful that we keep the continuity of our work coherent and that, since everything the camera sees becomes significant, we know the significance of everything we do. We need to understand what world the writer or filmmaker has put us into. And we have to choose our needs in order to be coherent within that world.

Every Picture Tells a Story

How a drama is shot dictates how we view it. Each director brings his or her vision to the subject matter by the way it is shot and edited. Whether people sit or stand, how their positions in the frame show their status, what is in and out of focus and how the filmmaker directs our gaze, affects what we take in and feel about the situation. 💿 **4.0**

Even the angle that the director chooses for the actors' gaze affects the way we view the scene. If you watch *The West Wing* (TV) you will find most conversations are shot at an angle that puts the actors' gaze quite a way from the camera. This gives us an objective viewpoint in keeping with the subject matter. We are asked to observe and draw conclusions. Occasionally, the series touches on a very emotional moment and then the actors' eyelines are closer to the camera so that we observe the characters in a more subjective manner. We become more emotionally involved.

Another thing that film grammar has taught us is that everything we see has an importance for plot or character. The choice of shot takes the viewers' eyes to the important component and everything seen acquires added significance. That means that you, the actor, have to have a good reason for your choice of props and your displacement activities.

I was directing a small scene about a married couple having an argument in the kitchen. The actor, in order to do something with his hands, started playing with a kitchen knife. When we played the scene back, it caused helpless laughter as the actor had inadvertently given us a murderous subtext that he hadn't intended. So you have to make sure that the props you choose further the story or give character clues. I don't mean that you can't use secondary activity in a naturalistic manner, but you do have to understand that the choice of props can affect the narrative of the film, so they must be part of the world that you inhabit and be coherent with your thoughts and feelings.

In the same way, any extraneous movements that are to do with your discomfort rather than the physical life of your role will appear magnified and begin to distract us as viewers. So, if your head keeps twitching for no reason, if you constantly scratch the side of your nose, or smack your lips – we will notice. If you want to use these movements, they will have to make sense within the life of your role. What follows in this workshop falls into the 'unnatural' part of our work that has to be learned until it becomes second nature.

Public versus Private

If we think of theatre as essentially a public medium – because of the interaction with an audience – then film is a private one. Almost all film is about a private world that we are allowed, as voyeurs, to see in to. Film is a 'fourth wall' medium. (In stage terms, 'fourth wall' means that when the actors look towards the audience, they see an imaginary fourth wall to the set.)

The most public act the actor can do within the public medium of theatre is to talk directly to the audience and break this fourth wall. In the private world of film, the most public thing that you can do is to talk straight into the camera lens because, by doing this, you are talking straight to your viewer – and the fourth wall disappears. If you are a newsreader or a presenter or are saying your agent's name at an audition for the benefit of the casting director, this is exactly what you want to do. In this instance, you look directly into the camera lens. But in a drama, it is very rare to engage directly with the audience like this and actors learn to avoid it. It is called 'spiking the lens'.

Of course, like all rules, it can be broken for effect. So, in a film like *Alfie* (1966 or the 2004 remake), the actor sometimes breaks out of the private world of the film to let us, the audience, know their unspoken thoughts. But it is a rare device and you should not look directly into the lens unless the director gives you specific instructions to do so. 💿 **4.1**

The Camera Bends Space

The camera has a way of bending space. So you have only to shift your gaze a little from the centre of the lens, even to the hard cover surrounding it, and you will then appear to be in your private world. If you look at a forty-five-degree angle to the lens, it will appear that you are looking at a much wider angle from it.

You will usually have your eyeline to the other characters set for you. But when you are thinking, don't be afraid to look close to the lens so we can read those thoughts.

Whatever takes your gaze on your fourth wall whilst you wrestle with your thoughts or whatever you see that sparks your thought – the tree outside the window, your reflection, the vase on the mantelpiece – can be put, in your mind's eye, in the direction of the camera. This is part of your film craft: to know where the camera is and what shot you are in. 💿 **4.1, 4.2, 5.5**

We can talk to someone for hours and barely glance at them. I was on a train the other day watching two men opposite me have a deep, involved discussion. The seating allowed them to look out front and, during six stops, they didn't look at each other once. If I'd had my camera with me, filming them in a tight two shot, I'd have seen what they felt about each other very clearly (as I did, sitting opposite them!). Yet, if I'd given that scene to actors, they would have probably tried to look at each other the whole time, and the scene wouldn't have had the same intensity as I'd have only seen them in profile. But if they had looked ahead, as my train companions did, I'd have seen the thoughts in their eyes.

If you are playing opposite another character and you would, genuinely, look down to hide what you feel, then that may be the right choice. But, whenever you can, think up or out rather than down. This is, anyway, what we tend to do in life, especially when we are visualising something. If the other character is behind or beside you, and you find yourself consistently looking down, it is more likely that you are subconsciously buying yourself space from the camera than from the other character. In your imaginary world, the camera doesn't exist, so be brave and look out into the distance and not to the floor.

If you have a prop to deal with – say, a newspaper you are reading, or a meal you are cooking – you may need to 'cheat' the position of the object when you are in a tighter shot.

Otherwise, your eyeline will be so low that your eyes will look shut, and we won't see your thoughts.

There are other strange phenomena created by the relationship between the lens and space. You will find that, in order for the camera to view you and another actor in mid-shot, you will need to stand really close together. As long as there is a little space between you, your relationship will look right. It means that you will have to stand too close for comfort to your partner, which can be unnerving until you get used to it. And the odd thing is that this shift closer for the tighter shot will not be noticeable when the film is cut together. The same applies if you are short and have to stand on an 'apple box' to be seen together in a tight two-shot. You would think that this change of height in relation to each other would register as unreal. But it does not. 🎞 **4.2**

You may have heard the expression 'crossing the line'. If two people are talking and you draw an imaginary line between them, a static camera would have to stay on one side of this imaginary line. If it 'crosses the line', the two people will appear to reverse their positions on screen, and this will confuse the audience. This reversed position would happen in life if you walked behind people, but because then we know that we have changed position, it doesn't produce a problem for our perception. But if you just see characters swapping places, the brain cannot compute the geography and it becomes very disorienting for the viewer. (Of course, very occasionally a director will 'cross the line' to do just that.)

These days, however, there is far less static camera work. Most films are shot with travelling cameras. That means that when filming a scene, the camera uses tracks or a dolly to move around the actors. Then, like life, it takes the audience with it on the journey, so the brain can adjust to the changing positions.

Coming into Focus

Film works like the eye. When you focus on one thing, the surrounding environment merges into the background and goes out of focus. This means that, in a close shot, the eye will see only what the director has decided is important and put into focus. The same has not been true of video, where everything in the shot appears to be on the same plane. These days, special lenses are being developed to combat this problem and it is claimed that some high-definition cameras can now match the quality of film. But if you are filming on a lower-budget video camera, you will see that if you stand in front of a drainpipe, it may appear to be growing out of your head! It also means that if you are playing a very small part in the background, you will want to keep your movements small and smooth, whilst they shoot the close-up of the leading actor in front of you. Otherwise you will be distracting. Of course, when you are in the foreground, you may do whatever you need to!

It's important to ask the camera operator what size shot you are in so that you'll know your parameter of movement, but on many shoots, multiple cameras are used, rather than just the one. This means fewer set-ups, as the same scene can be taken from lots of different angles at the same time. The actor may even be followed around by a steadicam, a camera with stabilisers that is strapped to a camera operator. It is able to take steady shots that don't have the same shaky quality that used to be associated with hand-held camera work.

If you are being filmed by a steadicam at the same time as being in a long shot, you can't really adjust the technical aspects of your performance. You just have to remain completely truthful and continue as you would in the master shot. The director will choose moments from this steady stream of closer footage to edit in later. In a way, it is easier as it releases you from having to be careful of extraneous movement in a close-up, and often results in a more fluid, naturalistic feel in the finished film.

Although you could be filmed from any distance, you will usually find the camera is closer to you on film than on video – which can be disconcerting if you're not used to it, and occasionally you can see a distracting image of yourself if you have to look into the lens for any reason (e.g. an aside to camera or playing a presenter). All the more important to keep your own imaginary environment clear and sharply focused in your mind's eye.

Shooting to Edit

The usual way of shooting a scene is to start with a master shot. This is a shot of the whole scene, which has to be on a lens long enough to see the whole action. Following the master shot, sections of the scene will be filmed by a closer lens in two-shot or three-shot format. By that I mean that two or three actors will be seen in mid-shot together. Unless the actors are really huddled together, this number of people is about all that can be contained within a medium shot. Finally, close-ups of the action and reaction shots will be taken. The amount of set-ups used in each scene will be dictated by a mixture of budget and the director's vision. 💿 4.7

It is worth remembering that if one person is driving the action, or telling another character some home truths, we want to see the other person's reactions. Sometimes the character on the receiving end – not saying or doing much but thinking and responding – becomes the most important role. The director may decide to add these reaction shots if you really keep listening and thinking (but not 'showing') during the master shot.

The editor will generally choose to cut from one size shot to another or to another part of the story on a physical action. So, once again, continuity of moves is important as these will be the cutting points. You will generally do a close-up from starting with a move from the master shot and the director will call 'Cut!' as you move out of shot or bring your cup to your lips. In a close-up, unless instructed otherwise, you simply go on to whatever action you set in the master shot and leave it to the director to decide when to stop. Don't make that decision yourself, as you never know what will be used in the edit.

You don't always know which camera is on you or what will be used in the final edit. So never go off the boil – the camera may be on you. Don't let your energy go during the long day's filming. You never know what parts of the mosaic the editor will use.

Shorthand for Shots 📀 4.6

ELS – extremely long shot
LS – long shot
MS – medium shot
MCU – medium close-up
CU – close-up
ECU – extreme close-up
EXT – exterior
INT – interior
SFX – special effects

(See my book *Acting for Camera: Truth 24 Times a Second* for a fuller list of jargon.)

Continuity

Once the master shot (usually the first set-up of the scene) has been done, your major continuity will have been set. Where you stand up and sit down, when you take a drink (and with which hand), and all your major moves will now have been recorded. In order for the scene to be edited successfully, you will have to stick to these moves in all subsequent filming. This means that when sections of the scene are done from different angles or with a closer lens, these moves must match. It is a good idea to get used to continuity and to become good at memorising it.

When you get sent off set for the relighting of the next set-up, it's a good discipline to write down what you remember of your moves. On any mid- to large-budget production, there will be a script supervisor on set to check continuity and, if everyone forgets, video playback can be used to check. But you will be highly regarded if you remember your own continuity and it will save everyone time and therefore money.

Within these larger moves that you need to repeat exactly, the little looks you take, the way you say the lines and the thoughts that govern them don't have to be identical. In fact they can't be – as you have to be freshly in the moment each time. Remember that they can only use one version so, providing everything matches where they want to make the cut, these tiny changes are fine.

It probably doesn't need saying that you mustn't change your make-up or unbutton your shirt between takes or set-ups. I was on a film once with a young boy in South Africa. His mother had been warned not to cut his hair, but one day, he clambered into the minibus to set with a smart closely cropped head instead of his usual curls. Apparently grandmother had visited that weekend and had been horrified to hear that he was filming with such unkempt hair and had taken matters into her own hands. The schedule had to be rewritten to move his important scenes and he had to be half-hidden in every shot for the next few weeks until his hair had grown again!

Finally, improvising or paraphrasing lines makes continuity hard. Try to be accurate with the script. I have been on too many films where the actors make up their own – it doesn't usually make it any better!

Continuity of Energy

One of the most important aspects of continuity is the continuity of energy. You need to have the same energy when you come to shoot the close-up at the end of the day as you had in the master shot at the beginning. Your need has to be as strong and you have to remember where you came from and with what urgency. You also need the same subtext.

I often see that in the master shot, the mood is light and the subtext is hidden, but by the time we come to the close-up, everything has become deadly serious and all the subtlety and humour has disappeared. Keep reminding yourself of your objectives and relationships and tempo.

Props

Props can be a wonderful thing to use when rehearsing. They can give a life and a specificity to your imagination. But when you come to filming, if you have a choice over your props, choose wisely.

Eating looks great on camera and has made memorable moments in films like *Babette's Feast* (1987), *Tom Jones* (1963), *Blow Out* (1973) and *Gosford Park* (2001). But you will find that dialogue through mouthfuls of food repeated on numerous takes is pretty hazardous. So, don't suggest food, but if you *have* to eat, at least choose food that's easy to swallow and take a tiny forkful.

Smoking is awful, as your cigarette will have to be replaced on each take to ensure it's the same length as it was on the one before. The same applies to the level of liquid in glasses or bottles. And, if you are drinking, it won't usually be alcoholic but it'll probably taste foul. If it is the real thing, then that brings its own hazards. John Mills in *Ice Cold in Alex* (1958) apparently had to do fourteen takes downing his real lager in one! Carlsberg later used it as a commercial!

Films are full of work-oriented roles: doctors, builders, gardeners, butchers, soldiers. You need to be able to use the tools of your trade expertly, but you have to use them as if you do so every day. When someone is expert with a particular instrument, tool or weapon, they have a firmness and dexterity about their movements. They don't necessarily have to give the task their full attention.

If an expert gives instructions, they sound assured and precise. The statement doesn't inflect upwards at the end as if they are asking whether what they are saying is right. And the words don't tail away at the end of the sentence. Penny Cherns at the London Academy of Music and Dramatic Art (LAMDA) devised an exercise where one actor shows a task in which they are expert and then another actor has to copy what the first did. This deftness of movement and strength of voice in the 'expert' is quite striking. In contrast, the other actor sounds hesitant and the movements are smaller with much less flair.

When you mix your famous cocktail with flourish and panache, there will be a special flick of the wrist that you give the shaker. The style will be uniquely yours. When you cut the garment, as you have for years, your scissors will fly with a deftness and ease. Whatever you need to do for your part, you should try to watch an expert at work.

You also need to be able to use technical names and any jargon or scientific terminology as if it is second nature. The drug with the long name that you hand to your patient must roll off your tongue. The instructions about warp-drive and laser guns that you issue to the crew of your spaceship must feel no stranger than the ones you used when you taught your nephew to drive. The botanical names for the plants that you proudly show from your trip to the Amazon must be as comfortable to you as the names of the items you buy in the supermarket – although they may mean more to you.

If it is possible, get hold of the actual items to practise with. If not, at least use something similar and make them so familiar to you that you don't need to think about them any more. You need to research by watching someone carrying out the work, whether live or on film, and by reading background material to understand the world you inhabit and then you must give your fingertips sense memory. Your muscles have to understand, not just your head!

In order for the audience to understand the narrative, you may be asked to hold important props higher in a close-up than you did in the master shot. So, for example, the gun (or the packet of detergent) may need to come up to your chest rather than your waist in the close-up for us to understand your intention. Amazingly, it will match when it is cut together and look natural in the framing. Always use props as silently as possible (see the section below on 'Sound').

Sound

You will remember from Workshop 3 that for most film and television, the sound mixer records sound on a separate track. These days it is usually stored on a hard drive. Your dialogue is recorded at the same time as the picture, but is kept separately for editing purposes and, if the quality is not good enough, it will be re-recorded in post-production. Background sound, music or special effects are put on later, as it would be very difficult to cut the picture from one shot to another with any continuous sound.

You will be recorded either by a sound operator holding a boom mic above you or, in a shot where that would not be possible, by a radio mic clipped discreetly to your clothing. It may sound obvious, but try to avoid hitting your microphone if you point to yourself when saying 'I' or 'me' or talk of love, and avoid your scene partner's microphone if you're telling them off. It is worth mentioning that, although your mic will be turned off when you leave the set, it will still be on between takes. So be careful what you say! The director and others will hear all your comments.

Some materials make radio mics difficult. Leather is notoriously creaky; try to avoid silk underwear as it rustles badly; watch out for jewellery. If you are dressing yourself, try to avoid hard-soled shoes or ask the sound operator to put felt on them. Otherwise you will drown out your own lines with the sound of your footsteps.

Which brings us on to noisy props – be very careful not to chop the onions vigorously or slam the door during your lines or anyone else's. It is amazing how noisy a knife and fork or a paper bag can be. So use props gently. If you have to throw something down in temper, you will have to resist throwing it as you say your line. You have to throw it before or after. 🔘 **4.5**

So it's not:

'Damn you, Perkins,' he says, *as* he throws the book down.

But:

He throws the book down. *Then* he says, 'Damn you, Perkins.'

Or:

'Damn you, Perkins,' he says, and *then* throws the book down.

You get the point! Otherwise you will have to do your lines later in post-production or a 'wild track' of the line will have to be taken after filming. A wild track is when sound only is recorded, and it is worth taking seriously, as these days the sound can be manipulated digitally to match your lip movements. Originally it would only be for editing guidelines but now it is often used in the finished production.

Remember, you can overlap with other actors when you are seen on the screen at the same time, but not if one of you is off screen. You need to keep the same flow, energy and rhythms as if you were overlapping but without actually doing so.

It is kind to use the volume that you will use in the take when you rehearse. If you whisper the rehearsal and then suddenly yell, it will not do the boom operator or sound mixer's ears much good!

Whispering is never a good idea. Even in the most intimate situation, add a little tone. Whispering is just 'white noise' and no amount of technical adjustment can give it tone. A very quiet voice rather than a whisper will give some resonance to your voice and therefore carry more emotion.

You need the amount of volume that you would use in life – and in life, it is usually more than you think. Keep the soundscape in your head if, later in post-production, music, engines or waterfalls are to be added. Don't talk 'past' the person or people you are talking to but make sure you are really communicating with them. If the director keeps mentioning that a word is getting lost, find a strong reason to say it and that will make it heard. And if the sound operator tells you that for some good technical reason you need more volume, believe it. Otherwise you will end up having to do it all again later.

Post-production

ADR (Automatic Dialogue Replacement), dubbing or looping is when you go into a small sound studio, many months after the original shooting and often in a different country to where the film was made. There you try to recreate your dialogue with the same intensity of performance and match the precise movement of your lips.

All the sections of dialogue that have either sound problems or where the director feels the reading could be better, are marked up carefully, and you will be given sheets with each cue itemised. You will normally be standing in front of the microphone, looking at the screen whilst the director and some technicians will be in the room with you. Sometimes they will be in a glass booth talking to you via your headphones or vice versa.

The relevant portion of the original filmed scene will be played for you (it used to be on a loop – hence 'looping'), and you will see a white line travel across the screen, hitting a marker when you are to speak. You can also be given an audio cue. You can choose to hear your original voice-track but most actors find this confusing, so I suggest you do this only if you find the synching impossible without this help. You can generally replace voice for a main role in a movie in a week or two, and usually you will work only for a couple of days.

Here is a short guide to successfully coping with ADR:

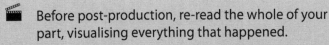

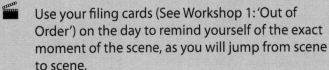

Before post-production, re-read the whole of your part, visualising everything that happened.

Use your filing cards (See Workshop 1: 'Out of Order') on the day to remind yourself of the exact moment of the scene, as you will jump from scene to scene.

If you were using another accent, you may need to redo your work on this – contact your original coach if you can.

When you are standing in front of the microphone, feel your whole body is involved. It is fine if you want to run on the spot to feel out of breath or anything else that you need to do. Be sure that you are standing roughly in the same way as in the filming and that you have the same energy.

Have all the same needs and pictures in your head that you had at the time of filming.

Be clear about the situation and specifics of the scene. Remind yourself of what you want the other characters to know and how much you want to hide.

Visualise the place and the person you are talking to. Really try to communicate with them.

You can put your hand lightly on your stomach to connect yourself up emotionally.

Round-up of Technical Tips

As Shakespeare should have said, 'Speak the speech, I pray you – and don't bump into the furniture.' It was good advice for theatre. For film, the list would have been somewhat longer. You have to hit your mark, know what size shot you are in, be aware of your radio mic and, if it's a moving shot, not bump into the camera. (Or a tree! 💿 4.8)

We have to accept that, in camera work, technicality rules. If the camera can't see something – it doesn't exist. The only reality is the reality shown on screen. In the end, only what survives the final cut will be used. You can work your socks off and give the best performance of your life, but in the end, if you picked up your glass with the wrong hand, turned away from the camera or had a piece of hair blowing in front of your nostril every time you breathed out, that take can't be used and won't exist.

If you don't hit your mark – or you do bump into the furniture or you forget your lines – you will hear 'Cut!' And you'll have to relax, breathe, think and go again.

If the camera breaks down, or the light gets too low or the sound mixer is seeking a mysterious hum, you will be left waiting for hours, hanging on to your performance. In theatre, I have only once seen a case where equipment held up the performance when a sophisticated safety curtain wouldn't rise. But in film, these technical hitches are an everyday occurrence. It's also worth hanging on to the thought that those twenty takes are invariably to do with the machines' performance, not yours.

But here are some tips to minimise your technical hold-ups:

- Find out what size shot you are in and therefore what your parameter of movement is. The camera operator will tell you. 📀 **4.6**

- Hitting your mark can be made easier with a few simple tips. Start where you will end and walk backwards, speaking your lines, back to the starting point. This will give you a rough idea of how many steps you will need to take. (Remember, we tend to take smaller steps when walking backwards.) Now check it again, going in the right direction using the same number of steps. Adjust and repeat if necessary. Try to see something fixed in your peripheral vision that will help you line up.

- If you need more than just a mark, ask for a 'sausage'. This is like a beanbag and your toes will feel when you reach it. Don't look down to find the mark. Know what stops you in your tracks and then merge your need to stop with these practical aids.

- Do any major move in rehearsal exactly as you will on the take. Get up smoothly as rehearsed to help the camera team. Stand up as proponents of the Alexander Technique advise – that is, without jutting your chin forward and by taking the weight on your legs.

- Be specific about your imaginary environment. Use the geography of that world to show us where the things you talk about are: the plant you are discussing, where you've come from, which shop you're going to, your father upstairs, and so on. 📀 **2.6**

- When holding, caressing or cuddling your partner, beware of patting, rubbing, tugging or pulling. These are often the ways that actors try to engender the feeling of a relationship on camera with someone they don't know very well. It isn't real and looks terrible on camera. Just hold the person, feel their warmth and caress them gently. 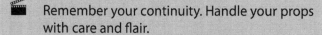 **4.4**

- Remember your continuity. Handle your props with care and flair.

- Use the same level of voice in rehearsal as you will on the take. It is very unfair on the boom operator and sound mixer to whisper on one take and scream on the next without warning them.

- Talk *to* your fellow actors – don't talk *past* them.

- When you hear the preparation ritual of 'Quiet, everyone, we're going for a shot', 'First positions', 'Sound speed', 'Camera speed', etc., prepare by dropping your breath into your centre, relaxing your shoulders and neck, flash up a picture of where you have come from and know what you want.

- When you hear 'Action!', let the thought form and then move or speak. Unless you are given specific instructions to do so, you don't have start immediately on 'Action!' Don't jump into your scene like a rabbit startled in the headlights.

- Know where the camera is and try to think in the direction of the camera, or we won't see those thoughts. Don't 'buy' yourself privacy from the camera by looking at the floor. We'll only see closed eyelids!

- In close-up (as long as it matches the master shot and your need), it can help to look away from your partner first as the thoughts gather, so that you are already in your imaginary world when the camera sees into your eyes.

- In close-up, concentrate on breathing before the camera turns, to stop twitching and nervous facial movements. If you are centred you won't overuse your face. Watch your feet are not shuffling or moving. Ground yourself properly; don't lock your knees. Feel your whole body is committed to the moment.

- In close-up, do not overlap lines with someone who is not in the shot as it makes editing afterwards difficult.

- Remember that in close-ups your partner will often stand so close than you cannot focus properly. You will then keep refocusing, moving between eyes, so try to favour your partner's eye that is closest to the camera. 4.1

- Blinking is another way of hiding. In life, we usually say important things without blinking. Learn to control the desire to blink more than is natural. 4.1

- If you wear glasses, when you remove them, you may be constantly refocusing or not focusing properly, which will be seen by the camera. Consider getting contact lenses as spectacles hide your eyes. 5.2

- Never 'cut' yourself (stop a take), unless you or someone else is in physical danger. You never know what part of the shot the director may want to use. After the take you can tell the director or script supervisor of any 'fluff' or mistake so it can be marked up and covered if necessary. Of course, things can go so horribly or funnily wrong that you all end up collapsed in laughter and the 'out-take' ends up as a DVD extra. But, given the vast expense of filming, always try to continue if you possibly can.

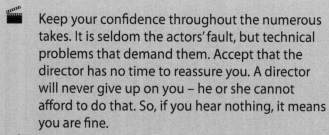 Keep your confidence throughout the numerous takes. It is seldom the actors' fault, but technical problems that demand them. Accept that the director has no time to reassure you. A director will never give up on you – he or she cannot afford to do that. So, if you hear nothing, it means you are fine.

Eventually, you will hear 'Moving on', and you will be on to the next set-up. Now you have to rest and then recharge to start from the beginning all over again in the next set-up, until you hear the final, welcome call, 'It's a wrap!'

Now watch Workshop 4 on the DVD.

Workshop 5

Off to Work We Go

Workshop 5

Getting the Work

We may fight that marketing term 'USP' (unique selling point). Most actors want to feel that they can play any part in any period and at any age, and, of course, they can. (Although, sometimes they can be their own worst enemies and be too fixed in their idea of themselves to dare!) Initially, though, most actors get interviewed for parts within their own age range and appearance.

That doesn't mean that you won't ever be asked to be in a range of different roles – from historical to futuristic, from princess to prostitute, from Australian to Yorkshireman. But when you do, you will need detailed preparation time to move into a role that is a long way from your habitual self. If you jump in too far and too fast at the casting stage, you are likely to descend into caricature. Remind yourself that it is you – you 'as if'. The casting director doesn't want the 'you' that interested them at the meeting to disappear when you read.

I reiterate again: you are unique. You are your own merchandise. Look objectively at yourself on a camcorder, in snapshots and when you catch an unexpected reflection of yourself. Don't be drawn to the things you don't like about yourself – the bumps, lumps and wrinkles. Look with a clean eye. If you were casting, what would draw you to this person? That is your USP.

There is a coda to this. Once you've done this, you must forget it, leave it alone and trust yourself. If you 'play' your USP, you will become a caricature of yourself. This is something that has happened to a great many movie stars who start out with something special but end up tiresomely exploiting this quality in every part they play. The best of them go through this patch and then become brave enough to let go and start again. You can't hang on to any tricks that have served you in the past. You have to rediscover your way to enter the specific, imaginary world of each role you play.

The Casting Director

The casting director is hired by the director or production company to find the right actors for the roles. They provide people that they feel will suit the brief. Most casting directors are very good at attending drama school productions, going to fringe theatres and watching showreels to hunt out new talent.

It's better not to send showreels to casting directors without asking first. And it's best to have one made up of real clips from wherever you can get them – film or TV appearances, student films, short films or interesting commercials. You can mix in workshop material too, but name it as such. It's always worth getting this material expertly edited and presented.

Try to avoid a company who package you up in a showreel of audition pieces they've filmed in-house. If you have no original material (or can't get hold of it), it's better to make a showreel yourself:

- 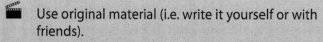 Use original material (i.e. write it yourself or with friends).
- Shoot it in real locations.
- Always use a separate mic (inbuilt mics aren't adequate).
- Record a 'buzz' track – a recording of the ambient sound of the location in which you are shooting, used to make the sound of the finished scene consistent.
- Make sure the editing looks professional.
- Call it a 'short'!

It's a good idea to write to the major casting directors whenever you are on television or on stage, as you can't always rely on your agent to remember to do this and a personal approach is often better.

The casting director is on your side! They want to seek out new talent in order to provide an interesting list of people for the director to see. And when you attend the casting, they want you to do well.

The Casting Process

Many actors find that, without a role to work on, they feel rather lost at auditions and much shyer as 'themselves'. I was watching one of my favourite singers being interviewed on a chat show and she appeared out of character – awkward and tongue-tied. In the course of the interview, she referred to the freedom that finding a 'persona' for a song gave her. When she performed at the end of the show, she was released, powerful and free. Using a persona in her performance had given her permission to use her tremendously powerful presence. But all her personas are simply aspects of herself that her imagination conjures up. So, if you find auditions nerve-wracking, you can find a suitable persona – such as you, 'the successful actor' – and prepare that role. **5.0**

  Use the exercise described in Workshop 1: 'Stepping into the Role'. This time see *yourself* at your most confident and successful, standing in the magic circle in front of you. Now take a step forward into *you* at your best.

 Anchoring: this is similar to the trigger work in Workshop 3: 'Triggering Emotions', and useful for confidence in interviews and auditions. Remember a time you felt extremely confident and when everything went well. It might be a moment of performance or when you achieved a sporting achievement or knew you looked stunning. Or the moment you felt a feeling of victory over someone or something. Again, relive those moments until you feel that glow of self-satisfaction and ease. Now create your own 'trigger' or 'anchor' by choosing the knuckle of one of your fingers and pressing there hard as you feel the emotion. In future, by touching that knuckle, you should recall a glimmer of that same sense of confidence that you buried there. This fusion of emotional recall and physical sensation acts as an anchor.

The first audition may be in the form of an interview or you may read with the casting director or the director. If it is a larger part in a film or television series, you may have a formal screen test with another actor. These days, there is a new development: actors are being asked to film the audition scene themselves. You can go into a small studio (there is one at the Spotlight offices in London, for instance) and record a solo screen test, which is then sent down the line direct to the casting department anywhere in the world. Or, with the increasing range of cheap video cameras, you can film it yourself. This saves the production company money on airfares – and helps their carbon footprint!

 If you are doing your own screen test, they do expect it to be propped and dressed as far as you can manage. Miming doesn't generally work on camera, so bring your wine glass, shopping bag, newspaper, etc.

 If you are using your own camera, use a separate mic on a stand near you rather than the inbuilt one.

In some European countries, such as Germany, scripts are sent to the actor to learn beforehand, and they are expected to give a polished performance at the audition. In the US and the UK, auditions are often of the 'cold reading' variety. That is, you are given the script when you arrive at the casting. If you are lucky enough to get a script before you come to casting, physically act it out at home to put the pictures into your head. Then learn it, but don't get 'patterned' as you may be directed into different choices. You need to learn it well enough to forget it. Sometimes you might be told not to learn it (in case your performance gets 'fixed'), but my advice is still to do so, but to hold the script. If you keep having to look down, then you will keep 'switching off' from the camera's gaze.

It is worth dressing and making decisions about your appearance based on the role you are being cast for. Don't go too far in this direction in case they want to consider you for a different role. But it is worth knowing how different you can look with different clothes, make-up and hairstyles. **5.2**

 When you are choosing what to wear, avoid white, black and clothes with stripes, checks or busy patterns. White can cause too much contrast with darker skin tones or hair, and if you are filmed against a white wall, you will disappear. If you wear black, it will soak up light and you will vanish against a black background. The checks and stripes may cause a 'strobing' effect when filmed on video. (**4.4** You will see Nadja's stripey blouse strobing a little.)

 At the audition, when you are given the script, be a detective. Pick out clues to who you are and what you want. When you begin, don't take a locking breath, visualise your partner and let your whole body echo your thoughts. You will often be sitting and won't be able to jump up when you want to as you'd be out of shot, but you can do subtle moves to allow you to follow your impulses. A slight turn or lean can say as much as actually getting up and walking away. Unless you have to reach for something, resist that impulse to lean forward!

 Take your time, look up when you can for the ends of sentences, and look at your partner when they are talking. Just look ahead at the script first to see your cue. If you know the lines, don't let your brain jump to the next one until you need to say it. Stay in the moment – don't know what you are going to hear or say next.

Remind yourself that they are not testing your reading. As Sanford Meisner said, 'Anybody can read. But acting is *living* under imaginary circumstances.'

Use the punctuation to show you where you have a new thought and dare to stop and breathe on the full stop. Suppose you have three sentences: 'Hello. Come in. Sit down.' Actors will tend to run them as one thought with a little lift at the end of each sentence that signals that there is another thought coming. In life we only have one thought at a time. For example (the thoughts are in italics):

Oh, it's you at the door – 'Hello.' *I'd better invite you in so you don't think I'm rude –* 'Come in.' *Oh hell, this is awkward –* 'Sit down.'

Or:

Oh, my love, you've come back – 'Hello.' *Can you ever forgive me? –* 'Come in.' *Please stay –* 'Sit down.'

Or:

Oh God, it's the landlord. He wants his rent – 'Hello.' *He's looking at the broken window –* 'Come in.' *I'll distract him –* 'Sit down.'

Or a million other ways. But only one thought at a time.
◉ **5.3**

That thought may come after a pause or it may crash-land whilst you are still speaking and form whilst the sentence tails away, but you can only focus on one thing at a time. And remember, thoughts and speech don't happen evenly at the same tempo.

If you tell a story in the role, you live through each moment. You don't jump beats. You tell each moment of your memory with the feelings it evokes. If you are happy at the beginning, then the listener doesn't know about the terror at the end until you get to it. Don't be afraid to use different voices when you relay what people said or to really yell or laugh. People echo the voices that they heard at the time. 📀 **1.1**

Audition Nerves

When you've done as much of the right kind of preparation as you can – that is, knowing everything you can about the situation, the people and the environment in your life and what you want – you will feel more confident. 📀 **5.4**

Don't forget to breathe! Use the breathing and voice exercises in Workshop 3: 'The Power of the Breath'. 📀 **3.1** The ones I use most often focus on energising the breath, getting vocal resonance and connecting up (📀 **3.1.a**), opening the emotional and vocal channel (📀 **3.1.b**), checking pitch (📀 **3.1.c**), and developing connection, confidence and projection (📀 **3.1.d**). 'The Seasons' breathing exercise is a great nerve-calmer. 📀 **5.1**

In the 'Brain Games' section of Workshop 3, there is the exercise 'Gathering the Chi', which is a great way to centre and increase your confidence. There are many other forms of gathering the energy around you, centring and calming yourself within the Chinese martial-art tradition. Here is another good centring version:

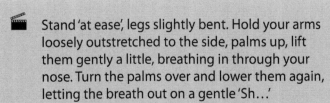

🎬 Stand 'at ease', legs slightly bent. Hold your arms loosely outstretched to the side, palms up, lift them gently a little, breathing in through your nose. Turn the palms over and lower them again, letting the breath out on a gentle 'Sh…'

🎬 After a few rounds, bring your arms in front of you, slightly bent and apart, palms loosely towards you as if you were holding an imaginary beach ball. Imagine this as a ball of energy. Keep your head lengthening out of your neck, release the tension in your shoulders. Hold this ball of energy for a few moments (don't get tense), then gently lower your hands back down to your sides. You will find you can gradually increase the time you hold your energy ball.

 You can find many examples of Tai Chi and Qigong exercises online.

Here's a final audition tip for the interview, which is a variant on my recipe for STAR quality ('Sit or stand up straight, Think And Remember to breathe'). It is based on a popular analogy, which I first came across in the work of business coach Michael Grinder. Under stress, people exhibit two different types of behaviour – there is 'cat mode' and there is 'dog mode'. The key is knowing which animal to use and when. In an audition, you are likely to default into your most comfortable animal type.

Dogs want to please and be liked. Dogs are social creatures and like to fetch on command and to gather information. They don't like making decisions, they prefer to be led. In dog mode, people lean forwards, nod their heads and gesticulate with their palms up. Their attitude says, 'You give me food, you give me warmth, you give me shelter – you must be a God.'

Cats want to do their own thing and to be respected for it. They are independent and make their own decisions. In cat mode, people sit back and watch and gesticulate with their hands palms down. Their attitude says, 'You give me food, you give me warmth, you give me shelter – I must be a God!'

By definition, actors tend towards dog mode, because they are in the business of empathising with others, they are sociable, they like people and they work as part of a team. Sometimes we need to turn our auditioning 'doggy' selves into cool credible cats. Instead of looking like a needy actor (or a dog trying too hard to please) – leaning forward, nodding, 'Yes, I can do that. I can bungee jump, I can water ski, I can jump out of the aeroplane without a parachute…' – sit back. Be friendly and fascinated, but fascinatingly cool. Turn your placating hands palms down. Feel strong and secure and say, 'That sounds really interesting, tell me more.' Take your space. You have a right to be there – offering mystery and bravery and just the right amount of 'attitude'!

Round-up of Casting Tips

- Choose your clothes for the audition to suggest the part, avoiding black, white and busy patterns.

- If you have time at home before the audition, act out any memories that your role talks about.

- When you only have a little time with the script, choose someone or somewhere you know for the people and places in the story.

- Sit back – don't lean forward. If you put your feet flat on the floor, you will feel more confident. Drive your energy from your centre. Keep your shoulders relaxed. Keep breathing.

- If you are going to be seen only in close-up, don't cross your legs – it throws your shoulders out of line and we won't have a master shot to understand why.

- Take your space – physically and vocally. Allow your whole body to echo your thoughts. Take your time.

- Hold your script high. Allow yourself to look up at the end of the thought. If you are listening, glance down to see your cue, then give your partner your whole attention.

- If you have learnt your script, you can hold it for an informal reading, but don't look at it. If it is a screen test don't hold it at all.

- Remember the environment around you in your imaginary world.

- For a screen test, use actual props. Film is a naturalistic medium and miming doesn't work.

- Know what you want and then try to get it. Know your relationships and status to others in the scene.

- Only use eye contact with your partner where and as you would do in life.

- Only have one thought at a time. *Don't know what you'll say next. Don't know what you'll hear next. Don't know what you'll do next.*

- You drive the thoughts, words and moves – they don't drive you.

- Remember, they actually want to give you the part! It will save them a lot of time and energy.

The Working Actor

'Three years at Drama School, five years in Rep, two years at the National and what do I get? "You 14th from the left with the mustache, drop dead when you hear the cannon fire."'

In any art, there is a symbiotic relationship between creativity and craftsmanship, imagination and technique. You want to operate truthfully within your imagined world, but at the same time you will work within the demands and constraints of your medium. Sometimes this might mean contorting your body into unnatural postures to keep your face in position for the close-up, flirting with a metal flag, or gazing into space and seeing aliens – and it will certainly mean standing too close for comfort. 💿 **4.2**

But in the end, it is the truthfulness that we will see. We won't know you are standing on a box, have a wire threaded through your underclothes or a man standing above you with a watering can. Neither will we know that your lines have just been changed, that you've had four hours' sleep or are suffering from seasickness.

They used to call it 'Doctor Theatre' because, in the moment of performing, everything else vanishes and you truly believe in the world you have created – like a child at play. And afterwards, you will feel exhausted but invigorated. That is why it is hard to wind down at the end of a long day.

You do need to learn how to rest between set-ups. By all means socialise with the cast and crew, but leave time for yourself. Take a book or music with you for long gaps. I wouldn't recommend trying to stay in your role all day. Any chance you have, lie down in your dressing room, trailer, the catering tent or just the grass. Lie down flat, rest your head on a book, knees up, feet flat on the floor (shoulder-width apart). Shut your eyes. And let your muscles release. It takes at least fifteen minutes to replenish the fluid in your spinal discs. Do some gentle breathing work. If you drift off to sleep, that's fine, as long as you know there's time to get fully awake again.

Then, when someone comes to check on you, do your psychological gesture, or chosen activity, remember where you've come from, where you're going to and what you want. Then start thinking as your role. And then you're ready and rested when they call for you on set.

When you get there, take the heat off yourself; take your energy outwards. If you find mnemonics helpful, use FLOW:

Focus
Listen
Open
Watch

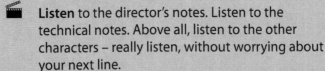

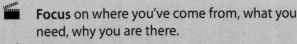

Focus on where you've come from, what you need, why you are there.

Listen to the director's notes. Listen to the technical notes. Above all, listen to the other characters – really listen, without worrying about your next line.

Open yourself up – your throat, your posture, your emotional channel. Let your energy flow outwards.

Watch the effect your words and actions have on the others around you – whether you do that openly or covertly depends on the imaginary circumstances.

Judi Dench says that you should take your job seriously, but not yourself. Keep a sense of humour both in and out of the role. You have to enjoy playing the game or there is no sense in doing it.

Checking the Monitor

I don't usually recommend looking at a monitor in between takes as it distracts you from your imaginary world and also wastes a lot of time. Some young actors get addicted to watching everything back, but I wonder what they are seeing – as only the director knows what will be used and how it will cut together. But sometimes you are asked to do something technically complicated that is hard for the director to explain. In this situation, you may be asked to view a take to help work out how to achieve what is wanted.

Sometimes it's the way that a shot is composed that dictates the style of acting. I was working with a young, talented actor

on location in an enormous cathedral in Sicily. She was playing a medieval girl wooed by a soldier, but now mourning at
the foot of his coffin. It was in the early hours of the morning
and we were running out of time. Once the sun rose over the
rose windows, we would lose continuity. The director asked
her to hold her arms high over her head as if beseeching the
gods. She was newly trained and desperate to remain naturalistic. No matter how many times we explained, she would
only produce tiny little movements, saying that the grand
gesture demanded by the director felt too extravagant and
unreal. Eventually we gave in and packed up.

I was always sorry that I wasn't able to persuade the director to let her see the monitor. What she didn't understand
was that the camera, far away from her at the furthest end
of this enormous building, was shooting a very long shot
and she was a tiny semi-silhouetted shape in a white shift,
holding up her hands to the vast vaulted space above. If she
had seen the set-up, she would have realised that what
seemed to her to be an enormous gesture was exactly what
was needed to tell any kind of story in that huge echoing
cathedral.

You have no choice, ultimately, except to trust the filmmaker.
But if you absolutely don't understand what is required,
then (once in a while) ask to see the monitor.

Corridor Acting

If you watch a television programme such as *Doctor Who*,
CSI, *The West Wing* or *Casualty*, you will see a lot of 'corridor acting'. The plot is pushed forward or attitudes to other
characters are shown as the doctors and nurses or police offi-
cers walk down corridors, holding clipboards or pushing
trolleys. Doors are pushed, equipment dealt with, as the
insults, flip remarks or flirtatious glances are exchanged.

These corridor scenes – showing characters going about their busy lives – are a writer's device to bring life and interest to plot-setting scenes or to have life-changing moments dealt with through passing comments. But it is surprisingly difficult to look as if you walk this corridor, street or flight of stairs every day of your life. So often actors look as if they are concentrating on how they walk. They look ungainly, stiff or bounce like Tigger in *Winnie the Pooh*.

You will also have to cope with hitting marks, keeping in line with the camera lens, trying not to clatter the props, and dealing with flimsy sets. You'll find yourself walking very close to the other actor, away from walls and door jambs that block you, and having to stop on a precise spot for a throwaway remark before you move on through the swing doors, checking your notes. And it all has to look completely spontaneous.

The secret is to get the geography and technical requirements thoroughly fixed in your head. And then to give yourself a real need to go where you are going. It may not be stated in the script, but know that you have to get that bedpan before Sister does the rounds, or take that X-ray to the doctor on duty before the patient reaches him, or get the car registration through to the duty desk before the shift changes. That stays as your priority, whilst you flirt, lecture or fight for your pay rise en route. The need to pursue these tasks may make you pause in your tracks, but not for long, because your feet are carrying you towards your objective.

You may be revealing a hidden secret as you operate on your patient, but your expert hands and eyes are still totally focused on your task of keeping that patient alive.

There are many BBC television scripts on the writers' development website (www.bbc.co.uk/writersroom) including several police and hospital dramas, which will enable you to practise your corridor acting.

Filming a Series

If you are in a series, playing a continuing role, you may have to deal with multiple scripts at a time. You may be not only shooting one story out of order but jumping from one story-line to another.

My tip from Workshop 1: 'You Work Out of Order' – to make yourself filing cards for each scene – will help you keep track of where you are in the plot/s! You may also find that as more writers come on board, adding new aspects to your role, you have to keep rethinking your needs and adding to your back-story to make sense of it. We are all aware of series that are excellent in the first instance but which, in subsequent series, get more plot-driven, with the characters losing coherence.

It is inevitable that new foibles and attitudes will be foisted upon you as the writers search for new storylines. Your task is to keep being specific and finding a way to make each new twist spring from some specific incident or attitude that has hitherto lain unrevealed. It is easy to start to coast but you have to be doing the same depth of preparation work for Series Seven that you did for Series One.

Cheating the Shot

Most of the examples of film and television mentioned in this book have had moderate to large budgets. If you are shooting something on a low budget or for a TV soap that needs to be shot really quickly, there will be fewer set-ups. You will tend to be in two- or three-shot framing.

This will mean being asked to 'cheat' the eyeline. Know where the camera is and make sure you think your thoughts and shoot your glances in that direction. When you do look at the other actors, remember to look at the side of their faces closest to the camera. Angle your feet a little so that you are not standing in complete profile to the camera. Stage actors do this all the time with the audience; you can make it second nature with a camera, whilst still staying in your imaginary world. 💿 **4.1, 4.2**

Terrible Dialogue

Once in a while, you will strike it lucky and have a marvellous script. Usually you will have a competent one. If you did a transcript of everything you said today, it would probably not be deathless prose. Nevertheless, I bet no one noticed. What they saw was you batting your way through the day, and all that it brought, in your own inimitable, unique style. In other words, 'it ain't what you say, it's the way that you say it' that matters most.

Sometimes, though, you do have truly terrible dialogue. The best route is to do all your usual work to make it specific and then just say it. If your reasons for saying it are strong enough, we will be listening to your intention as much as the words themselves. But if you really can't make sense of why you would say it, or the period or style seem completely wrong, talk to the director. If that isn't possible, then you can usually get away with little changes here and there or subtle paraphrasing. But once you've made the changes, you must be consistent or you will cause continuity problems. (Most directors are fine with a small amount of legitimate script-changing and most actors do it – but keep it for emergencies!)

You may find you have too much dialogue. This may be because it is an adaptation of a stage play – these are often wordier – or the writer is giving us background knowledge to further the plot. If it is really unwieldy, it is worth asking the director if some of it can be cut. A few snips can give you more time for thought. And thought works better on camera than dialogue.

But if it is one of those wonderful scripts, then your business is to find out why you say everything you say, rather than making life easy for yourself. I was workshopping a scene from one such wonderful script: Anthony Minghella's *Breaking and Entering* (2006). The prostitute Oana is having a conversation with Will about his desire to clean up the King's Cross area of London. She suddenly comes out with the phrase, 'This is the human heart. This is the world. Light and dark.' It is completely out of character and Will asks her if she found it in a fortune cookie, a remark she finds very insulting. The actor was having trouble with that line, so I suggested that it could be the lyrics of a song. Maybe they're on the CD that she has given Will that evening. Or maybe they were lyrics to a song she had written herself. Suddenly the words made sense and so did her extreme reaction to Will's light-hearted remark. So she did an improvisation of singing that song at home before coming out on the street and meeting Will, enjoying the words she had written. After that, the scene flew. It is worth digging out an internal reason for lines that don't come easily at first.

We are not always lucky enough to work with a writer like Minghella, but there is often more to be mined out of scripts than actors first believe. And your preparation is to mine it out. Most scripts are better than you think and better than your changes. You shouldn't make changes out of laziness or because the language isn't like your own habitual style. So before you start rewriting, make sure that it *is* terrible dialogue – and even if it is, that you're not making it worse!

Costume Dramas

Posture will be very important in a costume drama, when you're playing a character living in the past, with a different deportment, physicality and clothing. These days, we tend to carry our weight and energy in our legs. You see people shuffle along shopping malls taking the weight from one foot to another. They don't look as if they're going anywhere. You need to re-find those latissimus dorsi muscles, so you can move like a cat. The posture work from Workshops 1 and 3 are crucial here. **3.2** If you are walking to get somewhere, you need to stride out and swing from your hips. This is your usual method of locomotion. Unless you are playing a member of the aristocracy, life is physically harder than we can imagine.

If you lead a physical life, you need a physical voice. You may not use so much of the light, conversational tone that bubbles out of us so easily in our modern social lives. The way you speak will depend on the period and your role – if you are a warrior, sailor or farmer, you are probably concentrating too hard on staying alive to be concerned by social niceties. If you are at court in the seventeenth or eighteenth century, you may depend on your wit, the subtlety of your speech and the argument of your language to survive (as happens in *Ridicule* (1996), directed by Patrice Leconte).

If you are a woman, you may have to learn how to handle a crinoline, a skirt with a train (never walk too close behind someone with a train!) or a hobble skirt. If you usually wear flat shoes, you may need to practise wearing heels. If you are a man, you need to feel comfortable in a stiff collar. You may need to learn to tie a bow tie. If you are having a corset fitted (whether you're a man or a woman), try to keep it loose around the stomach area to help with breathing and digestion. Practise wearing something similar around the house to get into your role.

You obviously need to dig into the period to find your attitudes and social mores. But don't forget that our main drives of love and hate, jealousy and greed remain exactly the same in any period. So, it is still you 'as if'.

Beware of improvising – 'Okay' springs out with alarming regularity. Most actors don't even know they've said it!

Action Movies

Action movies are physically demanding. They are usually shot in a far-flung land, through many seasons, in mud and grit and fake blood. They involve much gruelling training and the acquisition of new skills like horse-riding, fencing and archery. They involve many, many takes that have little to do with acting problems.

There's usually not much dialogue to work with. I suggest you improvise some during your pre-production training whilst you are on the horse or firing the arrows, to find your voice and match it to your physical life.

Health Hazards

Film and television sets are frequently full of smoke, haze and – worst of all – paper snow. They are also hot, dehydrating and you are often swapping from day to night without enough rest.

Take care of yourself. Rest when you can, use steam at night if your throat feels tired, warm up and cool down, and drink any rehydration drinks offered.

The One-Day Job

It is difficult to do the odd day on an ongoing soap, series or long film. Everyone knows everyone else and is well established in their role. You are expected to come in, do the job smoothly and professionally without taking too much time, and then drive off into the sunset.

Approach it as you would any other job. Prepare thoroughly, especially with any props or business mentioned in the script. This side of it must not hold up you or the production.

Cheat some relationship rehearsals with the other actors if you have a chance to. Even if you are tired from travelling, take an hour in the hotel bar or pub with them if it's offered. If you do, you'll feel more relaxed with them the next day. If they are really friendly and you are supposed to have a close relationship, any hugging or touching – within the normal social rules – will break the ice and prepare you better for the scene ahead.

If it is a difficult scene (and you're very lucky!), you may find your scene partner is prepared to do a quick rehearsal, improvisation or line-reading. Don't be afraid to ask.

When you get on set, ask any relevant questions of the director. During the take, give yourself full permission to be there and take the time you need within the scene.

Accents and Dialects

Unless you are very confident with any new accent you are called upon to use, you may be offered time with a dialect coach. If the budget allows, the coach may be on the set to help you, but if they are not, beware of improvising, as that is when the accent is likely to slip.

Be careful that you don't take on non-specific, blanket assumptions with the new accent. Sometimes mannerisms and generalised character choices are tied up with our pre-conceptions of certain modes of speech and regional accents. You must be as specific and detailed in this area as any other.

Give yourself a practice sentence that takes you back into the right accent. Use it together with any warm-up that changes the placing of your voice every time you walk towards set. You can find a movement that feels right to accompany it.

If you have to do ADR later – try to recontact your dialect coach. If that's not possible, prepare thoroughly from your original notes and samples.

If you have to work on your own to acquire a new accent, there are some really excellent teaching tapes around by specialist dialect coaches that do more than give you samples of the accent. The ones I've found particularly useful (because I am generally teaching actors British or American accents) are those by Penny Dyer, Paul Meier, Allyn Partin and Gillian Lane-Plescia, but you will find others depending on the accents you need. *How to Do Accents* by Edda Sharpe and Jan Haydn Rowles (Oberon, 2007) gives a clear procedure to follow, and a wealth of source material. You can also find many examples on the internet: IDEA – the International Dialects of English Archive (www.web.ku.edu/~idea) is very good.

Those Tears Again

Everyone wants to be able to cry as needed (Workshop 3: 'Triggering Emotions'), but it is not necessarily better to cry real tears as you'll probably cry yourself out in the master shot and will need your red eyes brought back to normal between each take.

If the director wants to see tears and you are offered an eye irritant from the make-up department or glycerine tears, take up the offer gracefully. It is not 'cheating' any more than the wig or the lighting or the fact you are saying learnt lines! Anyway, like Pavlov's dog, when you feel that prickling in your eyes or the wet tears on your cheeks, you will probably cry anyway. It can act as a trigger!

Prosthetics and Extreme Physical Changes

It's worth mentioning that if you have to have extensive prosthetic work (oh, the early mornings!), you should give yourself a good facial workout and massage at the end of each day so that your muscles don't get tense.

If you have to be strapped into any new physical shape or contorted in any way, give yourself a good fifteen minutes after shooting to have a full body stretch and relaxation cooldown so you come back to neutral at the end of each day.

Extremes of Imagination

We've talked a lot about the importance of your imagination working overtime on set; how you need to people your world and have specific images for everything you talk about. The most extreme feat of imagination required comes when you work on Green or Blue Screen.

When special effects are going to be added later by CGI (computer-generated image) you will work against a coloured screen that ensures all objects of that colour will not be recorded. So, if you are standing in front of a green screen, everything green will disappear and if you have blue eyes, beware of standing in front of a blue screen, as they will vanish! These two colours are the most widely used as they are not usually part of our skin tones.

Against this background, the special-effects department will have marked where, later, they will put in the aliens, wild animals or mythical beasts. You will have to interact with these creatures, know exactly what they look like, have an attitude towards them and believe in them totally.

If you are very lucky, you may have a mock-up to work with, but it will often be a technician with a long pole rustling a tree or a metal flag for your eyeline.

I worked with a young actor in his first film where he had a dragon as his companion, from egg to a fully grown, rideable friend. We experimented with kittens and puppies as models, but they never stayed still, so in the end he had nothing but his own imagination. He drew the dragon at every stage and imagined how it felt, smelt and talked to him. As the voice would be put on later, he even had to create that in his head.

He had to play pretend games as if he was five again. But he also had to be very precise and make detailed notes as he was meeting his dragon friend at different sizes in random order over many months of shooting.

The Never-Ending Story

Long shoots can be very tiring if you have a leading role, and it is important to conserve your energy. Like being in any confined environment, things can get out of proportion. Make sure you spend time in the real world to bring back your sense of what's really important. It is worth reminding yourself what excited you about the role in the first place or the research you did for it from time to time, as it is easy to lose the original drive you had over a protracted shooting period.

If you have a smaller role, you will find yourself with extensive gaps between shooting. Whenever you go back to the project, prepare again with any games you found helped and by looking back through your card index (Workshop 1: 'You Work Out of Order'). Remind yourself of your objectives and backstory.

The Actor and the Director

Your director is not your Svengali; he or she will expect you to bring your own work to the part. Some directors may have come from an animation or special-effects background and not know how to help with your preparation. Others may inspire you to new heights. But they all have a right to expect that you will come to set fully prepared (without having decided *how* to play it), and that you are flexible enough to work in their way.

I have been on sets with free, secure directors who are happy to let their actors bring their own ideas. Equally, I have worked with directors who already have the set lit and the camera in position when the actors arrive. They know exactly where they want you to be, how you are to move, and will even tell you how to say the lines. In this situation, all your homework will stand you in good stead. Because in that split second you can decide exactly why you stand like that and what you are looking at and why that is the only possible interpretation you can give to the script.

You can, of course, offer your own thoughts and must – within the given framework – make the work your own. If you don't have a director used to working with actors, you have to decode his or her requests for an end result, and know what you want and how you feel that will lead to this conclusion. If, for example, the director tells you to shiver, you need to deal with the cold. If you are asked to cry harder, you must know why it hurts you more. If you get the instructions to look angrier, you have to up the stakes so you have reason to be furious.

You are only one element in all the ways that the director tells the story, and many approaches can lead to gripping dramas. Although you will probably be happier working with directors who allow you some flexibility and input rather than a dictator who will treat you like a prop to be inserted into the structure, nevertheless, in the end, you are being paid to fulfil your director's vision – whatever (within reason) that director's vision may be.

So, if you walk onto a lit set, with everything prepared and are told to kneel on one knee, hold your hand out thus and say the line with a particular intonation – it is your job to know why it has to be that knee, what you are reaching for and what you want. Everything is a circle. We've looked at how you can approach your part through the physical and the psychological. Although you would normally work forwards, organically, from the impulse to the action, you can work backwards from the action to the impulse that must lead to it. Even with the most organic director, there will be times when the technical constraints of filming mean that you have to work this way. But you are an actor and that's your job!

Making Your Own Movies

I suggest you get used to seeing yourself on camera and that you get together with a friend to film each other. As the hardware for making films gets cheaper and easier to use, so more and more actors will make short films and produce their own showreels. With a good camcorder and the computer software with which to edit, making a short film now costs about the same as putting on a theatre production on the fringe, and I foresee that actors will do this more and more as a way of marketing themselves. Director Marc Price claims he made his zombie film *Colin* (2008) for £45 – and it got a cinema release!

I was told a story about an American film producer/agent: in the nineties he used to get two thousand unsolicited film scripts a year from prospective writers and directors. Now he gets four thousand completed low-budget movies! Each filmmaker is hoping these will either be released or they will lead to a commission for a funded feature. There are two ways of looking at this: 1) That the crews and actors worked unpaid on four thousand feature films. Or 2) That these crews and actors got filming experience on four thousand movies. You can take your pick on how you view this new phenomenon – but both are true!

In the UK, Skillset (www.skillset.org) offers courses on filmmaking, training opportunities in practical skills, and general advice. You will also find many enthusiastic young filmmakers via networking websites like the international organisation www.shootingpeople.org.

What Kind of Film Are You In?

Films are made in many different styles – from comedy to tragedy, from period dramas to TV soaps, from action films to domestic dramas, from naturalism to surrealism. You may use dialects or heightened verse language, physical clowning or song and dance.

I think all these styles can be found within the 'as if' of your work. If you are in the court of Charles II, your gestures will be extravagant to show off your cuffs and your language elaborate to show off your wit. If you are an extremely physical person who acts before he thinks, and has to carry the chickens across a road in a cage without a fastener and doesn't notice the manhole... or the fox in it... you may appear to onlookers as a clown. If you have to use the warp-drive to get into hyperspace to catch the invading psychopathic Venusians – you will focus on clear action and not on subtext (and you will have been on a strict training regime to increase your muscles, which you'll be delighted to ripple to get the attention of the female pilot next to you). If the film is set in a dream world, you will live in a world of your imagination – which may torment you. If you are a super-being, you know your power will get you out of any trouble – so you'll have no fear or torment. And so on.

What you decide you need and the world into which you put yourself can help you feel real in any genre. If you burst into song, then you are singing your subtext, letting your lover know how you feel. Then you can return to social niceties when the song stops. If you are dancing and an orchestra strikes up in the middle of a city street, then you are dancing in your imagination – you have magically transported yourself to a world where there is a string band.

If you are taking an overdose of sleeping pills in a tragedy, you want to escape the cruel world, or you need to hurt someone, or you want to save someone pain. In a comedy you take them because you want to die looking beautiful, or you want to take them but you can't swallow them, or you take them and wait to die until you realise they were vitamin pills. The comedy can either be in the situation or because the action and the needs are incongruous. The situation can genuinely amuse you in the moment, but what you can't do is to decide that it will be funny to an imaginary viewer – because then it won't be!

Fine-tuning

Because I often run my workshops with very experienced actors, I am frequently working on fine-tuning. The camera acts as a microscope, so working on screen away from the pressures of filming can allow you to adjust minutely. A wonderful actor may still use a covering smile when under stress, or their eyes may not be quite as alive as when they talk about their real world. It doesn't matter where you are on your journey or how experienced you are, there is always room for fine-tuning. The camera allows you the joy of working on these tiny moments, catching that flash of thought and those subtle changes. The work is never done.

Stereotypes

'And this here is Maisie. She's got the looks, the charisma and a great pair of acting coaches.'

Actors want to work on roles that challenge them. We should fight stereotyping. Parts should be as well-rounded and surprising as people in the real world. Men can be caring and vulnerable, women can be brave and strong, the elderly can be carefree and daring, children can be sharp and wise.

Casting departments and directors should remember that many roles can be filled by actors of all ethnicities, genders and physical disabilities – doctors, lawyers, social workers, business people, thieves, writers, politicians, and so on and so on. Casting should not be limited by race, class, age or gender unless it is genuinely limited by the plot or the situation. Only then will we be surprised, challenged and delighted by the breadth, ambiguity and life unfolding in front of us on the screen.

Sadly, although things have improved, they have not improved enough. Women, particularly older women, have a hard time finding interesting roles at the moment in movies. Hollywood appears to have reverted to seeing women primarily as set decoration and dealing in stereotypes. European and independent movies are much better, but commercial cinema seems to be going through an action-based 'blockbuster' phase with little room for serious acting challenges.

Behind the scenes, it's even worse for women – so no wonder the good roles are so rare. According to Martha M. Lausen's 2008 study *The Celluloid Ceiling*, of the top-grossing 250 films made that year, 65% had no female executive producers, 82% had no female writers, 90% of them had no female directors and 96% of them had no female cinematographers!

Television drama can be better at providing actors with interesting work. Drama series such as *The Sopranos*, *The Wire*, *The West Wing*, *Wallander*, *The Street*, *Life on Mars* and *Our Friends in the North* remind us that, at its best, television can be even more powerful than film because the characters' lives are explored over a greater time scale. But our television quality, too, is threatened by lack of funding and commercial interests. It is imperative that dramas of artistic merit that deal thoughtfully with a range of topics continue to be funded. We want good plots about extraordinary ordinary people of all ages and without the need for botox and plastic surgery!

The only answer to this is to vote with our feet – or our remote controls – as an audience. And where we can, we should take control by making films about subjects that are relevant to us and writing roles that are interesting and relevant for all of us to play.

Action for Actors

Alfred Hitchcock once remarked that 'drama is life – with the dull bits cut out'. Film comes from life. It is a dream, a game of complicity and an entertainment. It has to have its own life, but it is not lifelike. It is life distilled and prescribed that, with the right magic, has suffered 'a sea change into something rich and strange'. And so you need to make rich, and sometimes strange, choices. ☉ **5.4, 5.5**

You can't learn acting just from reading a book or watching a DVD. You also have to do it. It is not enough to know; your body has to know. Drama schools teach acting but, even at their best, they can only help you to teach yourself, to take away the blocks and to help you learn the technique. They can teach you to do the unnatural – only you can supply the natural. The actor Herbert Lom said that Alexander Mackendrick, who directed him in the great Ealing comedy *The Ladykillers* (1955), told him that writing, directing and acting cannot be taught. It can only be learned through self-education. In other words – by doing.

Sample Scene Rehearsals

Scene 1: *The Silence* (1963) by Ingmar Bergman

Ester and Anna are sisters. They are travelling, together with Anna's young son, when they are forced by Ester's failing health to stay in a seedy hotel in a country that seems to be on the verge of war. Anna left her needy older sister and son to go out to a bar this afternoon, where she picked up a strange man. Ester is dealing with both the pain of her desire for her sister and her illness. 🎧 **4.0**

It is dusk. Anna has just told Ester she will go out again:

```
Ester has poured herself out a cognac.
She takes cautious sips.

                ESTER
   Where've you been all the afternoon?

                ANNA
      Taking a walk in the town.

                ESTER
         Where did you walk?

                ANNA
            Just nearby.

                ESTER
        That was a long walk.

                ANNA
   I didn't feel like coming back
            to the hotel.

                ESTER
           And why not?

                ANNA
     Just didn't feel like it.

                ESTER
          You're lying.
```

```
                    ANNA
            As if that mattered.

                   ESTER
         What've you been up to?

                    ANNA
        If you don't know, you're stupid.

    Ester falls silent a few moments, smokes
    her cigarette, looks out of the window,
    the scorn of her smile does not diminish.

                   ESTER
         Where did you find that man?

                    ANNA
        In the bar, just across the street.
```

I have included the directions in the printed script to give you a feel for the scene. In practice, I would advise you to delete those, as directions like that are for the reader not the actor. You can read them to help you 'play detective' when you first approach the scene. But you can't use a 'scornful smile' unless that happens to be the organic end result of what happens to you in the moment of playing the scene. Writers often describe the moods or actions of their characters. Only use them for your first reading and then forget them.

Work to Do on Scene 1

You need to read the script and then find out the differences between you and the role. What do you want? Where are you? What exactly is this hotel room like?

Impros

You need to establish relationships. For example:

They are young children. Ester could be bathing her younger sister's knee. She could kiss it better. Does Anna enjoy that? They hug.

They are teenagers. Ester is lending her best dress to Anna for her graduation ball.

Ten years ago Anna was pregnant. What were the circumstances? How does she tell Ester? How does Ester react? Has Ester had boyfriends? (The film does not tell you the answers but you need to have your own backstory.) Act out their conversations.

How has Ester spent the time in the hotel room whilst Anna was away? Act it out.

How did Anna meet the man in the bar? Where did she go? What made her come home? When did she decide to go out again?

Wants and Needs

What does Ester want of Anna? There are many possible answers: she needs to hold and make love to her. She wants her to stay with her. She wants love from her. She wants to let her sister know she knows what she gets up to. She wants the freedom to do as her sister does. She wants Anna to reawaken her desires by hearing her stories of her sexual encounters.

What does Anna want of Ester? Here are some suggestions: she needs to escape and find her freedom. She wants to forget her problems. She wants to hurt her sister. She wants to punish herself. She wants the physical relationship back that they used to have.

There are no right answers. That is why films and plays can be remade or revived many times. Each time there will be new questions and new answers. The actors will supply different needs that lead to new actions.

To do the *circling* work with needs:

Anna could take: 'I want to escape you.' Ester could take: 'I need you to love me.' Start by exploring a different action each time: to show love, to hurt, to plead, to cajole, to tease, to reach the other, and so on. Repeat the phrases to each other for at least five minutes. Use whatever space is available (don't keep the filming requirements in your head), and be as physical as you need to be (without endangering anyone!). Gradually, you will be drawn into the specific situation of the scene, having explored all the possible ramifications of your relationship. ☉ 3.8

To do the *circling* work with words from the text:

Ester could take: 'Where did you walk?' Anna could take: 'I didn't feel like coming back.' Repeat these lines until you have explored all the possibilities and are drawn back into the scene. Then Ester could take: 'You're lying' and Anna: 'As if that mattered', and repeat those for a while. Then change to Ester: 'What've you been up to?', and Anna: 'If you don't know, you're stupid.'

If you were rehearsing alone as Anna, you could imagine Ester standing by the window, glass in hand, and just keep repeating a need such as: 'I need you to let me go.' Getting no response will be a spur to try to get one by using any means possible. Or as Ester, you could imagine Anna sitting in a chair, her back to you, and keep trying the line: 'You're lying. What've you been up to?'

You can experiment with different needs and lines. You are trying to find key drives but every attempt will uncover something and push the work forward.

Now find your *psychological gesture*:

Ester's psychological gesture may involve some pleading or beseeching action. Anna's may be protective or defiant. Ester may be defending herself or tugging Anna towards her, or

Anna may be pulling Ester towards her. Only you will know through your body. No one else will play the role like you.

 Get a friend and a camcorder and film this scene. Make your world real for yourselves before you worry about the camera. Why has Anna come back? To see the child? If so – where is he? To get changed? If so, where is the bedroom? Is Ester drinking and, if so, what and where is the bottle? Share your territory. Is there a window? If Anna has come from outside, has she a coat and handbag? (Actors forget the real world when they do scenes. If you've come from outside, would you really have gone out without any possessions?) Is she doing something as she speaks – making up, putting away her keys?

 Now film it. Is the window towards the camera? Is Ester sitting where she can see the street as Anna comes in? If so, you can film it in one shot, as long as you find the right distance for Anna to walk round her chair to allow for height differences. How much does Ester need to look at Anna? Probably not much – so we can see both of them from the front most of the time. Mind those props – don't let them get noisy!

 Now try an experiment (every picture tells a story!). Film it with Anna sitting, having just come in, and Ester coming in from another room to fill her glass. Do the same moves but with reversed seating. Now, because she is behind her, Ester can look at Anna. But Anna may not need to look at Ester much. Play it back and see how it has changed the relationship and status between them. 💿 **4.0**

Scene 2: *Eternal Sunshine of the Spotless Mind* (2004) by Charlie Kaufman

Charlie Kaufman's screenplay is one where your 'out of order' cards would come in very useful. It crosses all kinds of timelines and has scenes that actually happen, scenes that are memories and scenes that might have happened or might happen. Clementine has her memories of her relationship with Joel erased from her brain, and when Joel realises this, he decides to have his memory removed too – but in the course of his treatment he rediscovers his passion for Clementine. The following scene is at the end of the movie. Some of the things Clementine says to Joel have been said before, such as telling him she is not a 'concept'.

Work on this scene as if it you didn't have any idea of the whole story – for an audition, for example. See it as a couple who have had a long-term, on-and-off relationship. It is set in the hallway to Joel's apartment where they have made love. Something has come between them yet again and Clementine is leaving. Last time they parted, they didn't see each other for ages, and if Joel doesn't stop Clementine, she will go for ever. She wants him to tell her he loves and needs her; he wants her to stay but can't say the right words.

```
INT. APARTMENT HALLWAY. DAY

Clementine walks down the hall. Joel
appears behind her.

            JOEL
        Hey, wait.

        CLEMENTINE
          What?

            JOEL
    I just wanted to...

He doesn't know what to say, stops.
```

                    CLEMENTINE
                      What?

                      JOEL
        I just wanted to... Um, I was just
      wondering... how your bruise is? From
               falling. Y'know?

                    CLEMENTINE
           It hurts. My ass is purple.

                      JOEL
       I'm sorry. It was a nasty fall. I mean,
      it was sort of funny once I realised you
                  weren't dead.

                    CLEMENTINE
           I'm good for a laugh, anyway.

                      JOEL
           No, that's not what I meant.

                    CLEMENTINE
     Anyway, look, I'm gonna go. Take care of
                   yourself.

                      JOEL
                    You too.

        She heads down the hall.

                     Wait!

                    CLEMENTINE
                      What?

                      JOEL
        I came up with another hair color.

                    CLEMENTINE
                  (not turning)
                   Oh, yeah?

                      JOEL
        Brown versus the Board of Education.

                    CLEMENTINE
       (walking, no change of expression)
           It's a little cumbersome.

> JOEL
> Wait.

She stops and turns.

> CLEMENTINE
> (impatiently)
> What, Joel? What do you want?

> JOEL
> (at a loss)
> I don't know.

> (pause)

Just wait. I just want you to wait for a
while.

They lock eyes for a long moment:
Clementine stone-faced, Joel with a
worried, knit brow. Clementine cracks up.

> CLEMENTINE
> Okay.

> JOEL
> Really?

> CLEMENTINE
> I'm not a concept, Joel. I'm just a
> fucked-up girl who is looking for my own
> peace of mind. I'm not perfect.

> JOEL
> I can't think of anything I don't like
> about you right now.

> CLEMENTINE
> But you will. You will think of things. And
> I'll get bored with you and feel trapped
> because that's what happens with me.

> JOEL
> Okay.

> CLEMENTINE
> Okay.

The End.

Work to Do on Scene 2

Firstly, of course, you need to know about this relationship. How did you meet? What broke you up the first time? How many times have you tried to make it work? I've given you your wants and needs – you need to make them strong. You need the love and passion to be enormous so that you have something to cover. Why can't Joel say the words he needs to say – has he ever used them before? If so, what happened? Or can he not say them because of his past, or because of the way she is? Why does she need to hear them? What makes her settle for what he does say?

What is the reference to the bruise? (In the film, they have visited the frozen Charles River that she loves to walk on in the moonlight and she has slipped.) Have they been walking on a frozen river? Or been skating? Or has she slipped on a wet pavement? It doesn't matter, but whatever you choose, you need to be specific. And if you have a scene partner, act it out. Then the bruise will be real (and funny) to you.

Mind the 'dot dot dots'! There are a few significant ones in this scene. Know what you would have said. Speak the sub-text out loud for this whole scene. Then bury it.

Make all the references specific and real to you. Find out what you mean about the hair colour, 'Brown versus the Board of Education'. (In the film, she keeps changing hair colour.) Could you be a writer? Could you be a copywriter for an advertising agency? Is that why she thinks she is just a 'concept' to you?

By making all these choices, you make a real life for yourself. If you meet the director and get given new facts, that's fine – you can change in an instant. But without this work you won't be a living, breathing person; you will be an actor standing outside the role, hedging your bets!

I love this scene. It is a classic corridor scene. Technically, you will keep having to move a short way and then stop again on your mark. And that stopping has to be because the force of your needs, or your reaction to the other person's needs, makes you stop. (But you have to hit your mark!) Joel has to stop Clementine by the power of his desire to stop her. But he can't use the words that will do it, so he has to keep finding other ways to make it happen whilst avoiding the issue. It is this inner conflict that makes the scene funny and moving.

There are three major beats which stop Clementine. Joel calls, 'Hey, wait', and stops her the first time. But he can't say the right thing so she walks away after telling him to take care of himself. He stops her again with his urgent 'Wait!' but she doesn't even turn and he still hasn't the courage to ask her to stay and, instead, talks about her hair colour. As she walks on he says 'Wait' one last time in a desperate attempt to get what he wants. But maybe he doesn't expect it to happen. Clementine turns to give him a last chance but she's running out of patience.

There is another beat when they lock eyes. Something has to happen to change Clementine's mind. To make her forgive his inability to say what he needs. She gives in, 'Okay.'

Joel's 'Really?' might be a sudden grip of fear because he's gone in too deep, or it might be relief or even genuine surprise that he's won. (You need to make that decision.) But Clementine won't give in without a warning and a proviso and he then reassures her.

There is a final beat when they make a pact to try again. 'Okay,' says Joel. 'Okay,' says Clementine. It is said lightly but underneath the words is a solemn vow to try again.

Whether it works out or not is another thing – Charlie Kaufman says that he wanted the audience not to know – but in this moment of time, the roles commit to each other.

There is so much in this short scene. You will uncover even more than I have offered. You have to bury your subtext and play as lightly as the roles are trying to do. But you can speak the truth through your eyes. *Don't know what to expect from each other. Don't know what will happen.*

 Now get a friend and a camcorder and film this scene. You will see how carefully it is structured and how you will have to film that structure. You will find that a tiny move with intention is all you need on camera. If you want to film it running down flights of stairs, you will be on a big-budget production with many set-ups. You can get the same effect with tiny moves and could do it on one master and a couple of close-ups if you keep the moves small, walk diagonally towards the camera, keep the intention to where you are heading, and if Clementine obeys the instruction not to turn. You will find these moves work symbiotically with the drives of the scene.

Scene 3: *The Constant Gardener* (2005) by John le Carré, adapted by Jeffrey Caine

Finally, here is another scene that I find exciting and challenging to work with. It is from the film *The Constant Gardener*, directed by Fernando Meirelles, who also made the stunning film, *Cidade de Deus* (*City of God*) (2002) using local children from the streets of Brazil.

Justin is a British diplomat working in Kenya. He met Tessa in London when she was attending a fairly dry lecture he was giving to lawyers. She is a student activist, fascinated by Africa and eager to uncover truths about foreign policy – especially in Africa. She is also fascinated by Justin and they have had a very brief affair. Now he is returning to Kenya.

```
INT. FOREIGN & COMMONWEALTH OFFICE,
LONDON. DAY.

The plant is in a window box outside
Justin's office at the FCO, an office
cluttered with packing cases labelled
'British High Commission, Nairobi' and a
profusion of books about Kenya.

Turning from the window with the excavated
plant, to lay it alongside others in an
insulated travel box ('Plants with care.
Do not expose to frost'), Justin finds
Tessa in the 12-foot-high doorway.
```

> TESSA
> Take me to Africa with you.

> JUSTIN
> (smiles)
> Rolled up in a rug.

> TESSA
> I'm serious.

> JUSTIN
> Yes, I can see that you are.

> (a beat)

> In what capacity am I to take you
> to Africa?

> TESSA
> I don't mind. Mistress, wife.

> (shrugs)

> Whichever.

Justin smoothes back the hair from his
forehead, the automatic posture he uses
when troubled or confused.

> JUSTIN
> Tessa, naturally I'm flattered...

> TESSA
> No! Don't even think about finishing that
> sentence. Yes or no?

> JUSTIN
> We hardly know one another...

> TESSA
> You can learn me.

Again the hair-sweeping gesture. A
moment or two, then:

> JUSTIN
> Then... yes.

He seems surprised by his own response,
like a man who has walked into a trap
only to discover as he springs into it
that it's one he has set himself.

> TESSA
> You will always protect me, won't you?

> JUSTIN
> Of course.

> TESSA
> And I you.

Work to Do on Scene 3

I'd like you to work on this yourself with a partner and see what you discover. Then film it. You should be able to film the whole thing in medium shot, but of course you could use a master shot and close-ups too.

Watch when Justin changes his mind or has the bravery to go with his emotions. What triggers that change? What looks, memories or feelings make it happen? What does her interruption – 'You can learn me.' – release in him? (He spends the rest of the film, which does not uncover the truth chronologically, trying to do just that.)

Don't miss the proposal. Does she know she is going to say that? Does it surprise her too? Does the agreement shock them both? (Without them being able to show that to the other.)

Once again, there is a pact at the end that becomes very important.

What do they need from each other?

Don't forget the plants. Are they simply a secondary activity for Justin or are they also emotional props? Things he can care for – in the way he will one day care for Tessa?

The notes on Justin's movements are there to give you clues about his inner state of mind. Take the intentions but play it your way, not just the way Ralph Fiennes played it in the film.

Resources

- Many film scripts are available to buy. You can also find lots of television and film scripts for practise online. Try www.script-o-rama.com for example.

- Many organisations run regular workshops on screen acting for professional actors and most of the clips on the DVD accompanying this book come from my workshops at:

  The Actors Centre, London
  (www.actorscentre.co.uk)

  The International Film School Cologne
  (www.filmactingschool.de)

  Interkunst e.V., Berlin (www.interkunst.de)

- Student films may be tracked down on indie sites like www.shootingpeople.com and www.indiefilmspro.com

- Information on films can be found at www.imdb.com

- Clips can be found on www.youtube.com

- And there should be somewhere to practise near you. I regularly add any workshops I'm doing to my website: www.melchurcher.com

Now watch Workshop 5 on the DVD.

If you return to the whole DVD at a later date, it will remind you of all the tips and exercises covered. Keep exploring!

5.6

And that's a wrap!

Please see page xxi for information on how to use the book and the DVD together.

If you are in the UK, Europe, Australia or another region requiring PAL format, please insert the disc into your DVD player with the PAL side up. If you are in the United States, Canada or another region requiring NTSC format, please insert the disc with the NTSC side up.

Introduction

Workshop 1: Keeping the Life

Workshop 2: Inhabiting the Role

2.0   Introduction

2.1   Light in the Eyes

2.2   The Picture in Your Head

2.3   Connecting with the Text

2.4   Missing the Moment

2.5   Being Specific {People

2.6   Being Specific {Environment

2.7   Dealing with Emotion {Personal Stories

2.8   Dealing with Emotion {Text

2.9   Building a Life

Workshop 3: The Physical Life

3.0   Introduction

3.1   Voice Exercises

    3.1.a   Energising Breath & Voice

    3.1.b   Opening the Channel

    3.1.c   Checking Pitch

    3.1.d   Connecting Up

3.2   Star Quality

    3.2.a   Sit Up Straight

    3.2.b   Instant Posture

3.3   The Actor's Toybox

3.4   Toybox {Binding

3.5   Toybox {Psychological Gesture

3.6   Toybox {Waking up the Senses

3.7   Toybox {Gesturing

(Don't forget to watch the credits to see the names and headshots of all the wonderful actors who appear on this DVD!)